Wai Lana's FAVORITE SOUPS

Wai Lana's FAVORITE SOUPS

Wai Lana Productions
P.O. Box 6146, Malibu, CA 90264
website: wailana.com
email: info@wailana.com

Printed in Hong Kong

ISBN: 978-1-932493-50-4

13 12 11 10 09   5 4 3 2 1

Food Photographer: *Michal Napierzynski*
Lifestyle Photographers: *Richard Lowther, Larry Olsen,
John Bishop & Katie Muncie*
Food and Prop Stylist: *Jana Gatien*
Home Economist: *Judith Grenier*
Layout and Design Director: *Cassandra Holmes*
Graphic Designers: *Michael Bond & Simone Bertschinger*
Editor: *Jana Gatien*
Nutritional Consultant: *Brandon Raynor, N.D.*

— Table of Contents —

Everyone Loves Soup

Nothing makes me feel cozier or more nourished than a warm bowl of delicious, wholesome soup. To me it's the ultimate comfort food and one my body craves all year round. The heavenly aroma of different vegetables, herbs, and spices simmering on the stovetop is like a warm invitation into the kitchen, enveloping anyone who walks in the front door—and luring people from all corners of the house.

A great soup is a nutritious symphony of flavors. It is strengthening, comforting, and versatile. It's something you feel good about serving to family and friends. Making soup for my loved ones, in fact, is a rewarding experience that makes me love cooking.

Soups for All Reasons

Whether hot or chilled, thick or brothy, chunky or smooth, classic or exotic, many soups make wonderful meals. For instance, Fabulous French Onion, Pasta e Fagioli, Vegetable Pho, or Hearty Chili needn't be served with anything else. Others, such as delicate Roasted Fennel Carrot Blend or rich Creamy Cashew Soup, make excellent appetizers.

Gentle on your digestive system, soups also provide amazing nourishment for your body. The Healing chapter, for example, shares delicious ideas to support different aspects of your health—be it weight loss or blood sugar.

In this book, you'll also find fun soups for kids—easy, foolproof favorites tailor-made for young tastebuds and growing bodies. There's also a delightful array of luscious one-pot curries and stews, as well as gourmet show-stoppers to knock the socks off anyone lucky enough to be seated at your table.

Soups can even be served as dessert, and anyone with a sweet tooth will fall in love with recipes like Sweet Rice and Berry Nectar. Indeed, this collection has a favorite soup to suit just about any crowd or occasion.

A Good Recipe Is Not Always Gospel

Since every palate is different, each style unique, and one's cravings as unpredictable as the weather, I encourage you to view each recipe simply as a guideline and to play with it, making adjustments to fit the season, mood, and moment. A good recipe is not always gospel—especially with soup, which is much harder to mess up than a soufflé! A truly good soup recipe is a formula you can follow and modify to your likes and dislikes. If you're not a fan of cilantro—my favorite—try fresh mint or Thai basil instead. If you don't have any yucca on hand, substitute potato. If you find a soup too thick for your liking, add a little more water, milk, or cream and be sure to adjust the salt as needed. If your vegetables aren't the freshest, add a stock cube to fill out the flavor of your broth. If you're not a garlic fan, omit it. Personal taste is a key ingredient in all recipes—and so are personal touches.

Being a casual cook myself who has learned from watching friends from all over the world add a pinch of this and a handful of that, I know that most soups are very forgiving. After all, I've been making most of these soups for decades without formal recipes, and though I sometimes swap carrots for parsnips or basil for thyme, they always turn out delicious.

Tried and Tested

On average, each recipe in this book has been tested five times—in addition to years of good use. Our team of 22 testers from all over the world tried the recipes to ensure that they are clear, easy to follow, simple to make, and, of course, really tasty. They also calculated the yields and times so that they're as accurate as possible. The recipes you'll find here scored the highest with the team and their families (well over a hundred people in total). I think the only exception was when someone made the Roasted Celeriac Parsnip Soup with celery instead of celeriac (it didn't have the same effect!). In most cases, however, you can play around with a recipe according to what you have on hand or stretch it out to feed last-minute company.

The Vegetarian Connection

As a longtime yoga practitioner, I've been living a yoga lifestyle—which includes a meat-free diet—for decades. I can honestly say that being a vegetarian has enhanced the quality of my life in countless ways. And, with sumptuous recipes like these, it's hardly an austerity! Nor is it inadequate nourishment. After all, my three healthy children have been vegetarian since birth and they are all accomplished martial artists and lifelong yoga practitioners— definitely not lacking in strength or stamina!

I truly hope this collection of favorite soups provides plenty of inspiration and delicious recipes to nourish you and your loved ones.

Wishing you the best
(and a very good appetite),

Wai Lana

Let these tips help you master the art of grocery shopping.

Get Your Basics

See Stocking Your Kitchen (pp. 6-7) and use it as a loose guideline for your shopping list. These items will give you a good foundation for soup-making and for healthy, delicious cooking in general.

Not All Produce Is Created Equal

Fruits and veggies vary greatly in quality and it can take a bit of experience to know how to pick the best. In general, select firm produce that feels, smells, and looks fresh. If you're not familiar with a certain vegetable, ask your grocer what he'd pick for his own family.

Stock Your Spice Rack

I like to buy my dried herbs and spices in the bulk section of health food stores (preferably busy stores, which tend to have a higher product turnover and therefore fresher spices).

Check Expiration Dates

It's good to check all expiration dates while you're in the store, especially when it comes to dairy products. It can be irritating to get home and realize you bought something that expired last week—and may even be risky if someone eats it.

Shop Locally

Local produce is usually fresher, tastier, and more enlivening for your body. Also, because it hasn't flown thousands of miles to get to you, it's much easier on the planet. Most cities have at least one farmer's market, plus an array of local fruit and vegetable stores. I highly recommend shopping at either to create the most flavorful, nourishing soups possible.

Explore

If you've never been to Chinatown or Little India or always wondered what's in that small Lebanese grocery shop you pass every day coming home from work—check it out. Any city with different ethnic communities is a wellspring of interesting and authentic ingredients from around the world. A wide selection of different curry pastes, chutneys, chili sauces, and other condiments abound in many small Asian shops and markets, as does an interesting array of vegetables, spices, and dried goods. So whether you like Indian, Chinese, Japanese, or Jamaican food, you'll be surprised by how easy it is to find the ingredients you often enjoy in your favorite restaurants.

Look Online

If you live in a small town where the odd ingredient might be harder to come by, look into ordering online.

You don't need to have absolutely everything on this list, but having most of these staples will prepare you for basic soup-making at a moment's notice.

STAGING YOUR KITCHEN

STAPLES

Basic Seasonings and Condiments

- A well-stocked **spice rack**

- **Salt** (I like sea salt, kosher salt, or Maldon, a gourmet finishing salt with a great flavor.)

- **Spike** (This is my favorite veggie seasoning salt. Others, such as Mrs. Dash, work fine as well, though I prefer the flavor of Spike.)

- **Bragg Liquid Aminos** (Here's a mild tamari or soy sauce-like condiment that lends excellent flavor to soups of all kinds. Use it interchangeably with tamari as they are nearly equal in sodium. You can find Braggs in many grocery and health food stores.)

- **Soy sauce** (I like Kikkoman) and/or **tamari**

- **Oil** (a good quality, bland cooking oil of your choice)

- **Oil spray**

- **Nutritional yeast**

- **Balsamic vinegar**

Broth Builders

- **Veggie bouillon cubes** or **powders**

- **Tomato paste**

- **Coconut milk**

- **Miso**

- **Unbleached white flour**

- **Corn starch**

You can also use sprinklings of dried potato flakes or quick oats to thicken or texturize a soup.

Veggies and Herbs

- **Basic soup veggies** (onions, garlic, ginger, potatoes, carrots, and celery)

- **Tomatoes** (fresh and/or canned)

- A selection of **fresh veggies** (like zucchini, beet, spinach, winter squash, broccoli, cauliflower, cabbage, yam, parsnip, turnip, fennel, baby bok choy, yucca, leek, etc.)

- **Frozen corn** and **peas**

- A few different **fresh herbs** (like basil, cilantro, mint, Italian parsley, dill, rosemary, thyme, sage, or tarragon)

AND CONSIDER HAVING AT LEAST A FEW OF THE FOLLOWING ON HAND AT ONE TIME ...

Legumes

- **Tofu** (you'll use mainly firm or extra-firm and occasionally silken)
- **Canned beans** (like kidney, black, or pinto beans, chickpeas, etc.)
- **Dried lentils** (especially red, brown, or green)
- **Frozen baby lima beans** or **soybeans** (edamame)

Dairy

- **Butter**
- **Cream cheese**
- **Parmesan cheese**
- **Milk** and/or **cream** (I generally use half-and-half)
- **Cheese** (like a good cheddar or pepper jack)
- **Sour cream**

The Grain Rotation

- **Rice** varieties (like basmati, jasmine, wild, and brown)
- **Pasta** (like orzo, ditalini, shells, fettuccine, or linguine)
- **Asian noodles** (like rice vermicelli, bean thread or mung noodles, udon, or ramen)

Keep It Interesting with ...

- **Vinegars** (like rice, apple cider, raspberry, sherry, balsamic, or champagne)
- **Toasted sesame oil**
- **Thai curry pastes** (like green, red, or tom yum)
- **Indian curry paste** (like Patak's Original Mild) or **curry powder** (preferably madras)
- **Nuts and seeds** (peanuts, walnuts, almonds, pecans, pistachios, cashews, sesame seeds, pumpkin seeds)
- **Fresh fruits** (apple, pear, mango, pineapple, berries)
- **Dried fruits** (cranberries, dates, currants)
- **Seitan** (found in health food stores and gourmet grocery stores)
- **Tempeh** (found in health food stores and gourmet grocery stores)
- **TVP chunks, a.k.a. textured vegetable protein** (found in health food, bulk, and gourmet grocery stores)
- **Vegetarian "meats"** (like sausages, chicken burgers/nuggets, or veggie meatballs—found in health food stores and many grocery stores)
- **Fancier cheeses** (like asiago, feta, gruyère, gouda, or brie)

If you're an avid cook, you're probably already equipped to make most types of recipes, soups included. But if you're just getting started in the kitchen, here's a list of valuable tools you'll find handy when using this book.

Chopping Boards

I like to have two chopping boards since I often have more than one thing on the go. Wood or marble is my preference. A big one is great for vegetables, while a small one is convenient for mincing smaller things like fresh herbs, garlic, and chili peppers.

Pots (and Saucepans)

A small (2-quart), medium (4-quart), and large (6- or 7-quart) will do you fine for making the recipes in this book. You'll probably use a medium pot the most. One quart is equal to 4 cups. Saucepans are also fine to use (they have one long straight handle whereas a pot has two short handles on each side). I like traditional, heavy, stainless steel, copper-bottom pots and saucepans, which cook things evenly, are easy to clean, and allow you to use less oil when sautéing. But really, most pots will do.

Skillets (a.k.a. frying pans)

Again, having a small, medium, and large skillet is ideal. If you're investing in only one for now, a medium-sized good-quality skillet would be your best choice.

Blender

I'm a blender person. They're not as messy as a food processor and they're easier to clean after use. I also find they purée foods to a smoother consistency. I'm sure there are many great food processors out there, but I'm sold on my 16-year-old blender.

Ladle

My favorite is a wide 1-cup (8-ounce) silver or stainless steel ladle. This way, when a recipe calls for blending 4 cups, you can measure as you ladle it directly into the blender. Wood or silicone are fine too; just be careful not to leave them lying around on your hot stovetop!

Good Knives

A good set of knives makes preparing food faster and far more pleasant. I've wrestled with several kabocha squash in my time and chopped a few stalks of celery—only to find that the knife had not severed the strings and that all my newly cut pieces were still linked together. Sharp, high-quality, stainless steel knives are a worthwhile investment and will last you a lifetime if you take care of them.

Spatula

A stainless steel spatula is best because it's nontoxic.

Wooden Spoons

I like to stir soups and stews with big wooden spoons. They not only fit the cozy, homestyle mood, but they're also gentle on your pots.

Slotted Spoon

For a couple of the recipes in this book, you'll find a slotted spoon useful for removing dumplings from boiling water.

Scissors

Scissors are great for mincing quite a few things in the kitchen: kaffir lime leaves, lemongrass, green onions, chives, nori sheets, and especially fresh chili peppers. I reserve a pair just for food prep.

Vegetable Peeler

The ideal peeler peels smoothly without removing too thick a layer of skin. You should be able to make vegetable ribbons with it.

Graters

A 4-sided grater will grate cheese, veggies, and zest. You may also want to invest in a specialized parmesan cheese grater, which now comes in many clever designs.

Zester

A fancy zester will give you long strands of citrus zest for beautiful garnishes. Not essential, but fun for presentation.

Mortar and Pestle or Electric Coffee Grinder

You can generally achieve more robust flavors if you grind your own spices. A mortar and pestle is my first choice, but if you haven't got one, an electric coffee grinder works great as well.

Colander

A nice, big colander is indispensable. I use mine every day for rinsing all kinds of vegetables and fruits and for straining pasta.

Measuring Cups

Aside from my set of stainless steel measuring cups, my 2-cup and 4-cup glass measuring cups always come in handy.

Fine Sieve

A fine-mesh sieve is useful for making panir (fresh cheese curd). It's also ideal for rinsing basmati rice, lentils, and other small grains and legumes.

Steamer

I like double- and triple-decker steamers, both Chinese bamboo-style and plain stainless steel. If you don't have one, a simple steaming implement that you insert and remove from the pot will do the trick for any recipes requiring steaming.

Roasting Pan or Dish

You'll occasionally need one for roasting veggies. I prefer ceramic or metal, but glass will do as well.

Toasting Nuts and Seeds

I use two methods for toasting nuts and seeds, depending on what size they are.

For small nuts and seeds, such as pumpkin, sunflower, and sesame seeds as well as pine nuts, I dry-toast them in a skillet over high heat. This is generally the easiest way to keep an eye on them. Once they get hot, stir constantly or shake the skillet. As they begin to crackle, some may pop, so be careful! If you like, season them with tamari, lemon juice, and cumin or chili powder. Once golden and slightly expanded, remove from the heat and transfer to a dish so they don't continue to darken or burn.

To toast larger nuts, such as almonds, pecans, and walnuts, you can use the oven or toaster oven—just be careful not to forget about them! You'll be less apt to burn them if you toast them on low heat (about 225°F) for a longer time, around 20 to 25 minutes. If your oven has a reliable timer, preheat it to 350°F. Spread the nuts on a baking tray, place them in the oven on a middle rack, and toss them once after 5 minutes. Bake for another few minutes or until the nuts are lightly browned and fragrant.

Tofu Possibilities

To me, tofu is like a blank slate. Malleable and versatile, it's a vessel for diverse flavors from all over the world. Whether you're in the mood for sumptuous caramelized teriyaki, a creamy low-fat soup, split pea soup with "ham," "chicken" noodle, or a spicy Thai curry, tofu can accommodate your craving. It is simply one of the healthiest and most versatile staples you can bring into your cooking. Each time you open a block of tofu, you open up countless possibilities.

Using and Storing Tofu: Before using tofu, give it a rinse and pat it dry with a clean cloth or paper towel. You can also slice the tofu into sections and wrap each piece separately to get even more moisture out. If you're not using the whole block, store the remaining portion in water in a sealed container and refrigerate. Change the water daily and it should keep for up to a week. You can buy tofu in bulk in many Asian and health food stores. Rinse bulk tofu with water and store it as described above.

Cutting Tofu: For soups, I usually cut tofu into tiny cubes. When I'm making tofu as a side or main dish, bigger cuts like triangles, rectangles, and "fingers" are nice. As with most things, smaller cuts make for quicker cooking. Just make sure you drain tofu well—otherwise it will release a lot of water when cooked. (This isn't a huge concern when you add tofu directly to a soup, but when you simply pan-fry or bake it, you may wish to drain it a little more thoroughly first.)

Tofu Varieties: Tofu is available in many textures, such as silken, soft, medium, firm, and extra-firm. But there are also deep-fried, smoked, broiled, and pre-seasoned varieties. The recipes in this book generally call for firm, extra-firm, or silken. Tofu is usually sold in 10- to 19-ounce blocks. Depending on the size it's cut into, 4 to 5 ounces of tofu amounts to about a cup.

Zesting Citrus Fruits

Unless you're preparing a long curlicue zest as an elegant garnish (which requires a special zester from a kitchen store), use the finest side of a traditional 4-sided grater or a small manual grater that is especially made for grating zest or hard cheese. Be sure not to grate too deeply into the skin; otherwise you'll hit the bitter white pith—and the pith can ruin your recipe! Once you start seeing white below the skin, you know you're grating too hard or deep. Move on to a different section of the fruit.

Garlic

Crushing and Peeling Garlic: I use a large chopping knife to crush garlic. I just place the garlic clove under the flat side of the knife and firmly but carefully press down with the base of my palm. This releases the flavor and breaks the skins, making the garlic cloves easy to peel. You can also crush garlic cloves with a rolling pin or use one of the effective and inexpensive garlic peelers and presses now found at many kitchenware and department stores.

Roasting Garlic: The process of roasting garlic really takes away its pungent edge. After an hour in the oven, garlic becomes soft, mild, and buttery—almost like a vegetable rather than a concentrated seasoning. To roast garlic, preheat the oven to 375°F. Take a thin slice off the top of the whole bulb to expose the cloves. Place the head(s) in a baking dish and brush the cloves with a bit of oil and a splash of Bragg Liquid Aminos (both optional). Add a little water to the dish, making sure the garlic sits in about ⅛ inch of water. You can also top the garlic with sprigs of fresh thyme or rosemary. Cover and bake for 60 to 80 minutes. Remove from the oven and allow the garlic to sit uncovered until cool enough to handle. Then squeeze the cloves out of their skins and use as desired. Not only is roasted garlic great in soup, but it's also delicious smeared on warm French bread with butter or on a crostini under melted cheese (see p. 286).

Preparing Lemongrass

Of the three best chefs I know, each has a completely different method for preparing lemongrass ... and each works fine.

- Nora crushes lemongrass stalks with a rolling pin, adds them whole, then removes them just before serving.

- Nadia slits a stalk lengthwise—twice—then ties it in a tight knot to release the flavor (this works only with fresh, moist lemongrass). She also removes lemongrass just before serving.

- Diana crushes stalks with the flat side of a knife, then roughly chops them into 3-inch segments. Usually we just remove them ourselves! I like this method because if you have leftovers, the lemongrass continues to infuse its lovely flavor.

There is no right or wrong, and depending on what kind of mood I'm in, I'll pick any one of these methods. For brothy soups I generally use Nora's or Nadia's method. For blended soups, I use Diana's and just go ahead and blend the lemongrass with everything else—this makes for a fabulous full flavor. Just be sure to peel away the tough outer leaves first, then use only 3-4 inches of the tender white inner leaves, just above the base.

Kaffir Lime Leaf

Don't be intimidated by the exotic kaffir lime leaf—it's very easy to use. You can add the leaves whole, like bay leaves, or you can remove the central vein with scissors, then finely mince the leaves. When adding them to a soup that you intend to blend, simply de-vein and blend them with the other ingredients. Kaffir lime leaves range in size from that of a fat thumbprint to that of a lemon. You can find them in Chinatown and Asian groceries as well as in some fresh produce markets and gourmet grocery stores.

Roasting Bell Peppers

Preheat the oven to broil. Slice the peppers in half, remove the seeds and membranes, and place them cut side down on a baking tray on the top oven rack. Broil for about 2 to 4 minutes or until the skins begin to blister. Remove from the oven and cover with a dish towel (this will make them sweat so that the skins just slip off). When they're cool enough to handle, remove the skins. If using homemade roasted peppers in a soup, add 1 tablespoon balsamic vinegar to the soup and increase the salt to taste.

Peeling Celeriac

When you peel celeriac (also known as celery root), use a sharp knife to remove about ¼ inch of the tough, gnarly skin; otherwise, you may find unpleasant woody fibers in your soup.

Salting Eggplant and Zucchini

A bitter eggplant or zucchini can ruin even the best recipe. So have a little nibble before tossing it into the pot to see if it passes the taste test—you can bet that if it's bitter raw, it will be bitter cooked. To remove any bitterness, sprinkle eggplant or zucchini pieces with salt, toss, and let them sit for 10 to 15 minutes. Rinse before adding to your recipe. As a bonus, these vegetables will now absorb less oil while cooking. There is no need to salt Asian eggplant.

Broccoli Stems

Unless broccoli stems are unusually woody or tough, I nearly always use them along with the florets. Just peel and trim the stems with a sharp knife to make sure there are no tough fibers. Add the stems to a recipe about 5 minutes before adding the florets as they take slightly longer to cook. I like the texture of broccoli stems because they are substantial but not starchy.

Lovely Leek … Beyond the Pale

I've never been one to use only the white portion of a leek. When it comes to soup-making especially, there is ample time for leeks to soften and impart their lovely flavor. I'll use up to ¾ of a leek just as long as it's cleaned well. Younger, smaller leeks are generally tender further up the stalk than the more mature ones. Old or young, tender or tough, the whole leek stalk can be used when making broth.

Preparing Fennel Bulb

To prepare fennel bulb, remove the outer layer if it seems tough and cut in half lengthwise with a sharp knife. Remove the dense core and place the fennel flat side down on a cutting board. Slice it as you would an onion, then chop the slices (or leave them long if you prefer). If your fennel bulb has long top stems, take a little bite to test them. Sometimes they can be woody and fibrous, making them unfit for eating. But you might find them pleasant, tender, and suitable for your recipe. The feathery green tops also make an attractive garnish.

Hot Chili Peppers

The many colorful varieties of chili peppers range from mildly warming to fiercely hot. Some are long and skinny, some are short and thick, and others are minuscule, wrinkled, or round. You can choose from fiery shades of yellow, orange, and red as well as green and even pink. Let your personal heat preference (or threshold) come into play when selecting a chili for your recipe. My favorites are the spicy little Thai chilies, which come in red and green and impart a fresh, peppery flavor—especially when added at the end. You may wish to start, however, with milder chilies like anaheim or pasilla.

General rule of thumb: the smaller the chili, the hotter it is. Also, the longer a chili pepper cooks, the more heat it loses, so if you want flavor *without* heat, add chili at the beginning of a recipe. Here's a list of different chilies and how they fare on a heat scale from 1 to 10 (10 being the hottest).

Anaheim, poblano (2-3)
Pasilla (3-5)
Jalapeño, chipotle (smoked jalapeño) (5)
Serrano (6-7)
Thai (7-8 … my favorite)
Scotch bonnet (9)
Habanero (10)

Chili Alternatives: If you don't have any chilies on hand, Tabasco sauce scores around 6 on the heat scale, while red chili flakes are about a 7. Most Mexican chili powders rate about a 2.

Preparing Dried Chilies: A smoky, spicy, dried chili—like chipotle, serrano, or anaheim—is a great way to add heat and depth of flavor to your favorite recipes. To prepare dried chilies, bring 1 cup of water to a boil over high heat, add 1 to 2 fresh chilies, cover, and boil for about 5 minutes to let them soften. Remove from the heat and let the chilies soak in the water for another 5 to 10 minutes. Pour the water and chilies into a blender and blend until smooth. Add this mixture to your recipe. Most often, however, I'll blend 1 or 2 canned chipotle peppers with ¾ cup water and 2 teaspoons of adobo sauce—no need to boil.

Fresh Chilies: Nothing burns your eyes quite like the forgotten residue of a fresh chili pepper on your fingertips. When chopping fresh chilies (or soaked dried chilies or even preserved chilies), I suggest wearing gloves or holding the chili pepper by the stem and mincing it with scissors. If you do touch the chilies directly, wash your hands well with soap and water and be conscientious about not touching your eyes for a few hours as the heat can sometimes linger, even on clean hands.

What Is Yucca?

Also known as cassava, yucca is a delicious tuber that's been used for countless centuries in tropical regions of the Americas. Perhaps better known for the byproduct derived from some varieties (tapioca), yucca is subtly sweet, hearty, and delicious in its own right. It has a dark brown, woody bark and a long, almost yam-like shape. Its smooth, cream-colored flesh is slightly denser than potato. It doesn't store all that well, so select pieces with no soft or black spots, keep it refrigerated, and use it within a week of purchase.

To prepare: Remove the bark with a sharp knife or peeler. Slice it in half lengthwise, then remove and discard the tough cord that runs up the center. Chopped into bite-size pieces, yucca takes about 15 to 20 minutes to cook when boiled. Be sure to cook it thoroughly. Yucca can be boiled, baked, or fried. It makes an exceptional mash with butter, salt, pepper, and a spoonful of horseradish.

Selecting Winter Squash

In my experience, small-to-medium, funky-shaped squash are tastier and sweeter than larger, more perfect-looking ones. They also seem to have a more desirable texture—more buttery and dense, rather than stringy or mealy. The kabocha is my favorite of the winter squash varieties, though it can be a little labor-intensive because it's so hard to slice. You'll need a *great* knife (or a great arm) to cut it with ease!

(My friend Diana—who has an impressive veggie garden—will split the bigger, tougher squashes she grows with a clean hatchet!) Softer for slicing and slightly quicker to cook, a smooth, sweet butternut, acorn, or Hubbard squash also works nicely in most soups. The skin of many winter squash can be eaten, though keep in mind that blending a dark-skinned squash into soup may turn it a less-than-lovely color.

Washing Vegetables

Most grocery and health food stores sell natural vegetable washes that make it easy to clean fresh produce, both organic and non-organic. They help remove pesticides, herbicides, fungicides, microbes, bacteria, parasites, and dirt. I also recommend rinsing vegetables and fruits with *purified* water, especially when preparing raw food.

Peeling Pearl Onions

A handful of the recipes in this book call for pearl onions, which can take a little while to peel. To speed up the process, drop them in boiling water and blanch for 30 seconds. Remove with a slotted spoon and allow them to cool for a minute or two. When cool enough to handle, they are a cinch to peel.

Peeling vs. Scrubbing Your Root Veggies

Whether or not you peel vegetables is really a matter of personal preference. Essential nutrients and fiber are abundant in veggie skins, but often so are pesticides, herbicides, and fungicides if your produce is non-organic. In general, I prefer to scrub thin-skinned potatoes like red, white, new, and yukon gold, while I definitely peel the tougher, sandy-skinned russet baking potatoes—at least for making soup! I recommend peeling non-organic carrots and parsnips. If your veggies are organic and clean-looking, however, keep the skin—it may be the most nutritious part of many roots. You can find an adequate vegetable scrubbing brush at any grocery, kitchen, or dollar store. I use the kind that can also be used for scrubbing pots and pans (though I use my vegetable brush for veggies only).

Cutting Different Vegetables

There are countless shapes and sizes in which to cut your veggies. A smaller dice makes for quicker cooking, while larger pieces are ideal for long-simmering winter soups and stews. It's really a matter of preference. You may wish to keep in mind that both Ayurveda and Chinese medicine recommend cutting vegetables smaller and cooking them more quickly in summertime, while in winter it's advised that foods be chopped into larger pieces and cooked longer to collect warmth. If it suits you, use such guidelines to tailor your soups to climate and season.

Grinding Your Own Spices

If you don't replenish your spices regularly, you may not get the full flavors you're hoping for. In fact, cumin, fennel, coriander, and mustard produce the tastiest powders when freshly ground with a mortar and pestle or an electric coffee grinder. I even have two coffee grinders: one for my morning flax seeds and the other for grinding spices.

Before grinding, however, it's ideal to toast your spices to bring out their flavors. Place the seeds in a small dry skillet over high heat for a minute or so until they darken slightly and begin to release their fragrance. Shake the pan or stir them constantly. Some seeds may expand and pop, so stand back an arm's length! Remove from the heat and transfer them immediately to your mortar, coffee grinder, or another dish. Allow them to cool for a minute, then grind them into an aromatic powder that will enliven the flavors in your soup.

Chauncing Spices

The process of chauncing is an intrinsic part of Indian and Thai cooking. It involves briefly sautéing seeds and spices in hot oil or ghee over high heat. This quickly releases fragrances and flavors. Add the bigger seeds first, smaller ones next, and powders last. The whole chaunce should take a minute or less. Add these spices to soups, curries, and stews to take them to another level of deliciousness. Believe it or not, if you begin to choke on the fumes, *this* is the sign of a good chaunce, especially when hot chilies are involved!

Salting Soups

Salting is a personal thing. The recipes in this book give you a good starting point. You it may find the amounts just right, or you may want to add more salt to taste. It's up to you.

Each salt measurement is based on fine sea salt, which is smooth-tasting and easy to dissolve. Most commercial sea salts have the same sodium content as table salt (iodized or non-iodized), so you can use them interchangeably. In addition to regular salt, many recipes call for Bragg Liquid Aminos, which is a full-flavored liquid salting agent that's great for making broths of all kinds. Soy sauce is also a staple, especially in the Asian Soups chapter. I find Kikkoman soy sauce tastes best. Tamari makes a great wheat-free alternative to soy sauce as well. Just to make conversion easy for you: A scant ½ teaspoon fine sea salt is about equal in sodium content to 1 tablespoon soy sauce or 1½ tablespoons Braggs or tamari.

Sodium Content of Different Salts
(mg per teaspoon)

Sea salt	2325
Coarse sea salt	1320
Table salt	2325
Kosher salt	1120
Spike	644
Cajun seasoning	600-1000
Bragg Liquid Aminos	220
Soy sauce	301
Low-sodium soy sauce	100-277
Tamari	335

Pre-mixed vegetable seasoning salts are also a wonderful way to salt your recipes while giving them a fuller, more complex flavor similar to that added by veggie bouillon cubes or powders. I like Spike, but other varieties should work fine as well. If you want your recipe to have a bit of a kick, you can also use salted Cajun, Mexican, or curry seasonings to taste.

Quickly Enhance the Flavor of a Soup

If your veggies seem a bit limp or dull-tasting, your soup may need a little help in the flavor department. If this is the case, you can always add any of the following:

- A veggie bouillon/stock cube (or a spoonful of powder); reduce the salt accordingly

- A tablespoon of miso (use light miso for creamy soups); reduce salt accordingly

- A splash of vinegar (either balsamic, apple cider, sherry, or champagne)

- A few tablespoons nutritional yeast

- Several splashes vegetarian worcestershire sauce

- For Asian soups, a couple of spoonfuls of hoisin sauce and/or rice vinegar or your favorite Thai curry paste

Blending Tips

- Most blenders hold 5 to 6 cups, so if you're blending an entire soup—often between 8 and 12 cups—you'll need to blend it in 2 or 3 batches.

- Never fill a 5-cup blender with more than 3 cups of hot soup. Always make sure the lid of the blender fits tightly, and hold it down firmly with a hot pad just in case some hot soup escapes.

- When you're blending only a portion of the soup, make sure to get a well-rounded mix of ingredients in each batch.

- If you're blending a soup in more than one batch, return the blended soup to the unblended portion and use a slotted spoon to get the rest of the chunks for the next batch. Otherwise, have a second bowl or pot ready to hold the blended portions of soup before they're returned to the pot (though this does make for more dishes to wash).

- Begin to blend first by pulsing the soup on the lowest setting for about 5 seconds, just to get it going. Then bring it up to the highest setting and blend until smooth.

- If using a glass blender, never fill it with cold water just after blending a hot soup as the glass may crack.

- When you're in a hurry or your blender's not working, try using a handheld immersion blender directly in the pot. This works well when a soup needs only to be *partially* blended. You *can* blend an entire soup with a handheld blender, but it won't be quite as smooth.

Thickening a Soup

If you feel your soup needs to be a tad thicker or creamier and you don't want to add anything fattening:

- Use a cornstarch paste. It should be three parts water (room temperature or cold) and one part cornstarch (e.g., 3 tablespoons water per 1 tablespoon cornstarch). Combine well with a fork until a smooth paste forms. Stir the soup constantly as you add the paste to prevent a large lump from forming. Add the paste gradually; you may not need all of it. The soup will thicken quite quickly. Don't add powdered cornstarch directly to the soup because starchy lumps will immediately form—and they're tricky to get rid of.

- Use a paste of half unbleached white flour and half water (e.g., ¼ cup flour with ¼ cup water). Combine until smooth and add to the soup as needed, stirring constantly.

- Add dried mashed potato flakes. For an 8-cup soup, stir in ½ cup at a time, waiting a few minutes for it to thicken before adding more.

- Add quick oats to achieve a nice, full body and texture. Sprinkle in a few tablespoons at a time, allowing them to thicken before adding more.

Lowering the Fat Content

Many soups in this book are not especially high in fat. But if you're strict about your fat intake, you can always lower the fat content by sautéing veggies in 1 tablespoon oil instead of 2, using oil spray instead of oil, or skipping the sauté step altogether. In recipes that call for half-and-half (cream), try using whole milk instead. In blended soups, replace cream cheese with silken tofu—but don't expect it to taste exactly the same! You may wish to increase the salt slightly to taste and add a tablespoon of eggless mayonnaise for a little more richness.

Ingredient Measurements

Because vegetables vary so much in size, I usually give cup measurements for recipes (e.g., 2 cups chopped carrot or 4 cups cubed butternut squash), sometimes with a secondary measurement in units as a helpful guideline (e.g., 1-2 carrots or one 2-lb squash). But always go with the cup measurements if there is any discrepancy.

Vegetable Sizes

When a secondary measurement in a recipe says 3 potatoes, 2 carrots, 6 tomatoes, and so forth, it refers to medium-sized vegetables, not jumbo or miniature ones.

Chopping Vegetables

For most vegetables, "chopped" means roughly cut into bite-size pieces, though garlic and onion will be relatively smaller. "Cubed" means bite-size cubes. "Diced" is a small chop. "Minced" is an extremely fine dice. "Julienned" means cut into thin matchsticks. "Slivered" means sliced into thin strips.

A Quick Sauté

Many recipes begin with a quick sauté of the onion and garlic and often a few other veggies as well. This releases and softens their flavors. A pot of soup also benefits from a little bit of oil. If you're looking to cut down on time, steps, or fat content, you can omit this step.

Times

Preparation times were averaged from our tester results. Although everyone moves at a different speed, these times should give you a ballpark figure on how long a recipe takes. Take note that prep times and cook times often overlap, so the total time is rarely a sum of the two.

Yields

Yields are approximate but have proven fairly accurate because of the cup measurements.

> **Soups are very forgiving**, so if you have an extra ¼ cup carrot or 2 tablespoons chopped onion left on your cutting board, feel free to toss it into the pot as well.

Classics

Whether you crave French onion, matzoh ball, or chicken noodle, you'll find these soups are just as delicious when made vegetarian.

Cream of Asparagus

This is a delicate soup that makes the absolute best of springtime asparagus and fresh tarragon, which are great together. Though it's a gorgeous appetizer for just about any savory meal, it's also lovely as a spring lunch or dinner accompanied by Smoky Tempeh (p. 291) and a peppery green salad.

Procedure

1. Heat the butter or oil in a 4-quart pot over medium-high heat. Add the leek, onion, and garlic and sauté for a few minutes until they begin to brown.

2. Add the water, celeriac or potato, and bouillon cubes, raise the heat to high, cover, and bring to a boil. Reduce the heat to medium and simmer for 10 to 15 minutes or until the celeriac or potato is tender.

3. Place the soup, half-and-half or milk, flour, and mustard in a blender and blend until smooth, in batches if necessary, then return to the pot.

4. Add the asparagus (except the reserved tips), salt, pepper, thyme, and tarragon. Increase the heat to high and bring to a boil. Reduce the heat to low, cover, and simmer for another 10 minutes.

5. Meanwhile, prepare the garnish. Heat the butter or oil in a small skillet over medium heat, add the reserved asparagus tips, leek, and salt, and sauté for a couple of minutes until just browning. Add the water and sauté for another minute or so until dried up. Remove from the heat.

6. Remove the tarragon and thyme sprigs. Blend 4 cups of the soup if you wish or leave it as is. Ladle the soup into bowls. Garnish with the sautéed asparagus and the pecans (optional) and serve.

> **Hands-on prep time:** 20 minutes
> **Cook time:** 30 minutes
> **Total time:** 40 minutes
> **Makes** about 8 cups

Ingredients

1 Tbsp butter or oil
½ cup finely sliced leek
1 cup chopped onion
1 Tbsp minced garlic (2-3 cloves)
5½ cups water
2 cups peeled, diced celeriac or potato (2 potatoes)
2 veggie bouillon cubes
1¼ cup half-and-half (cream) or whole milk
¼ cup unbleached white flour
1 Tbsp dijon mustard
3 cups chopped asparagus* (about 1½ bunches; reserve tips for garnishing)
1½ tsp salt or to taste
Fresh-ground black pepper to taste
2 sprigs fresh thyme (or 2 tsp dried)
6-8 sprigs fresh tarragon (or 2 tsp dried)
2-3 Tbsp chopped toasted pecans** for garnishing (optional)

Asparagus Tip Garnish

1 Tbsp butter or oil
Reserved asparagus tips
½ cup finely sliced leek
¼ tsp salt
¼ cup water

*Cut off and discard the tough, woody bases of the asparagus.

**See Toasting Nuts and Seeds, p. 10.

Potato Leek Soup

Anyone who's tried this soup never leaves so much as a drop in their bowl! It's a warming, comforting chowder filled with pleasing flavors and textures. If making it a meal, go with the tofu option; you'll find the extra protein makes the recipe quite substantial. I like to serve it with a platter of balsamic-splashed roasted veggies.

Procedure

1. Heat 2 teaspoons of the butter or oil in a 4-quart pot over high heat. Add the onion and sauté for a couple of minutes until it just begins to brown. Add the garlic and sauté for another minute.

2. Add the water, half-and-half, potato, celery, turmeric, pepper, and 1¾ teaspoons of the salt and gently bring to a boil. Immediately reduce the heat to medium-low, cover, and simmer for 10 to 15 minutes until the potato is tender.

3. Meanwhile, if including the tofu, heat 2 teaspoons of the butter or oil in a medium skillet over medium-high heat. Add the tofu and ¼ teaspoon of the salt and pan-fry for about 5 minutes, stirring occasionally, until the tofu is golden on most sides. Once the potato is tender, add the tofu and corn (both optional) to the soup.

4. In the same skillet, heat the remaining 2 teaspoons butter or oil over medium-high heat. Add the leek and the remaining dash of salt and sauté for a few minutes until the leek begins to brown. Add this to the soup along with the rosemary.

5. Simmer the soup for a few more minutes. Remove from the heat, ladle into bowls, garnish with toasted almonds (optional), and serve.

Tips/Variations

Blended variation: To achieve a thicker consistency, blend 2 to 3 cups of the soup before adding the tofu, corn, and leek.

> Hands-on prep time: 20 minutes
> Cook time: 25 minutes
> Total time: 35 minutes
> Makes about 8 cups

Ingredients

6 tsp butter or oil

1 cup chopped onion

1 Tbsp minced garlic (2-3 cloves)

2 cups water

2 cups half-and-half (cream)

4 cups cubed yukon gold potato (3-4 potatoes)

2 cups chopped celery plus leaves (4 stalks)

⅛ tsp turmeric

Fresh-ground black pepper to taste

2 tsp salt plus dash or to taste

1 cup finely cubed extra-firm tofu (optional)

½ cup frozen corn (optional)

1½ cups finely sliced leek (2 leeks, white part only)

1 tsp dried rosemary (or 2 tsp minced fresh)

¼ cup toasted sliced almonds* for garnishing (optional)

*See Toasting Nuts and Seeds, p. 10.

Amazing Cream of Mushroom

Here's a robustly flavored, satisfying chowder that lets you savor the diverse shapes, soft textures, and deep, woodsy flavors of hearty, protein-rich mushrooms. Rustic yet elegant, this recipe is a foolproof crowd-pleaser.

Procedure

1. Melt the butter in a 4-quart pot over medium-high heat. Add the onion, celery, leek, and garlic and sauté for a few minutes until they begin to brown. Add the mushrooms and sauté for a few more minutes.

2. Add the remaining ingredients, increase the heat to high, and gently bring to a boil. Reduce the heat to medium, cover, and simmer for 10 minutes or until the potato is tender. Remove from the heat.

3. Place 3 cups of the soup in a blender and blend until smooth. Return to the pot and stir through. Ladle into bowls and serve.

Tips/Variations

Presentation: If you have a few leftover mushrooms, sliver and sauté them briefly in butter or oil over medium-high heat. Garnish each bowl with a few slices.

Hands-on prep time: 15 minutes
Cook time: 20 minutes
Total time: 35 minutes
Makes about 8 cups

Ingredients

3 Tbsp salted butter
1 cup diced onion
1 cup chopped celery (2 stalks)
1 cup finely sliced leek (1-2 leeks)
1 Tbsp minced garlic (2-3 cloves)
4 cups mixed mushrooms*
  (like cremini, shiitake, and oyster)
  (1 pound)
6½ cups water or Mushroom Broth (p. 283)
2 tsp salt or to taste
2 cups peeled, diced potato
  (2 potatoes)
2 Tbsp sherry
Fresh-ground black pepper to taste
1 tsp dried rubbed sage
  (or 1 Tbsp minced fresh)
1¼ cups half-and-half (cream)

*Rinse the mushrooms and discard any tough stems. Tear or chop the mushrooms into bite-size pieces. You can also use other mushroom varieties like button, porcini, and chanterelle.

Matzoh Ball Soup

Matzoh ball soup is a classic Jewish recipe that's usually made with chicken stock. Being vegetarian, I had never tried it until my friend Lalita made a batch of her veggie version to prove it could be done—and done well. Upon trying it, I was sold immediately, but it was my kids who really loved it. With tender, savory dumplings floating in a flavorful golden vegetable broth, this wholesome recipe is perfect for tastebuds of all ages.

Procedure

1. Heat the oil in a 4-quart pot over high heat. Add the onions and sauté for a few minutes until brown.

2. Add the celery, water, carrot, ginger, thyme, dill, salt, and pepper and bring to a boil. Reduce the heat to medium-low, cover, and simmer for about 20 minutes. Meanwhile, prepare the matzoh balls (see next page).

3. Increase the heat to high, bring to a boil, and add the matzoh balls to the soup. Boil for 1 minute, then remove from the heat. Gently stir in the parsley (optional), ladle into bowls, and serve with 4 to 6 balls per bowl.

Tips/Variations

Richer broth: To enhance the richness of your broth, add a few tablespoons nutritional yeast and/or 2 vegetarian chicken bouillon cubes instead of salt (then add salt to taste if needed).

If you don't think you'll finish the whole pot, add just enough matzoh balls to the soup for now, reserving the rest for later. Store leftover soup separately from leftover matzoh balls. When you reheat, bring the soup to a boil over high heat, add the matzoh balls, and boil for one minute. This way, the matzoh balls won't break apart during storage.

Hands-on prep time: 25 minutes
Cook time: 30 minutes
Total time: 40 minutes
Makes about 9 cups soup plus 24 matzoh balls

Ingredients

1 Tbsp oil

1 dozen whole pearl onions,* peeled and trimmed

1 halved onion

2 cups chopped celery
plus leaves (4 stalks)

10 cups water

1½ cups chopped carrot
(2-3 carrots)

⅓ cup minced ginger

1 tsp dried thyme

½ tsp dried dill

2½ tsp salt or to taste

¼ tsp black pepper

¼ cup minced Italian parsley
(optional)

1 recipe Matzoh Balls (p. 32)

*See Peeling Pearl Onions, p. 16. If you prefer, you can use 1 cup chopped onion instead.

Get to Know Gluten Flour

Gluten flour is very useful in vegetarian cooking because it makes a great coagulant and texturizer for eggless baked goods and dumplings, such as matzoh balls. A natural protein found in wheat, gluten creates a chewy texture that also makes it a popular foundation for meat substitutes like seitan (a.k.a. wheat meat and wheat gluten). Containing 75% protein, gluten flour has fewer calories and carbs than most other flours.

Matzoh Balls

Ingredients

¼ cup oil
½ tsp celery seed
1 cup Cream of Wheat (farina)
1 tsp minced garlic
¼ cup minced Italian parsley
½ cup matzoh meal*
½ cup gluten flour**
2½ cups broth (from the soup)

Procedure

1. Heat the oil in a large nonstick stainless steel skillet over high heat. Add the celery seed and cook for 30 seconds. Add the Cream of Wheat and garlic and toast for another minute, stirring constantly.

2. Add the parsley, matzoh meal, and gluten flour and stir for a few seconds, then add the broth. Stir constantly until the ingredients come together in one big mass of dough. Remove from heat and cool to touch.

3. Divide the dough into 6 parts and make 4 ping-pong-ball-size dumplings from each part.

---

*Matzoh meal can be found in the kosher section of most grocery stores. If unable find it, use crumbled saltine crackers instead.

**You can find gluten flour in health food stores—both prepackaged and in bulk.

Fabulous French Onion

A few years ago, my family and I tried this soup when having dinner at our friend Nadia's house. She used pepper jack instead of gruyère cheese, as well as sweet vidalia onion and pear. It was rated a 10 by everyone at the table—and an 11 by my son. You'll have to try it yourself to find out why it could perhaps be the best French Onion recipe on the planet. I personally can't imagine following this soup with an entire dinner. Try serving it as a cozy meal with Smoky Tempeh (p. 291) over an elegant mesclun salad tangled with oven-roasted fennel.

Procedure

1. Heat the butter in a 4-quart pot over medium heat, add the leek, onion, and garlic, and sauté for 30 to 40 minutes, keeping them covered most of the time and stirring occasionally until the onions caramelize. Add another tablespoon of butter if necessary.

2. Once the onions have caramelized, add the sherry and simmer uncovered for a few minutes to let the alcohol evaporate. Add the water, salt, thyme, pepper, and soy sauce, raise the heat to high, and bring to a boil. Cover, reduce the heat to medium-low, and simmer for another 10 minutes, then remove from the heat.

3. Meanwhile, preheat the oven to broil. Spread the slices of bread on a baking sheet and place under the broiler for a minute or so, then turn them over to toast the other side. Remove the bread pieces from the oven and butter them.

4. Ladle the soup into ovenproof bowls and top with 2 slices of bread, 2 to 3 slices of pear (optional), and ½ cup or so of cheese. Broil for a couple of minutes until the cheese is bubbly and golden, then remove from the oven. Garnish with toasted almonds and dried cranberries (both optional) and serve right away.

Hands-on prep time: 30 minutes
Cook time: 1 hour
Total time: 1 hour 15 minutes
Makes about 8 cups soup plus bread and cheese

Ingredients

6-7 Tbsp salted butter
plus extra for bread

1 cup sliced leek (1-2 leeks)

5 cups slivered mixed onions
(red, brown, and/or vidalia)

1 Tbsp minced garlic (2-3 cloves)

⅔ cup sherry

8 cups water

2 tsp salt or to taste

1 tsp dried thyme

Fresh-ground black pepper

2-3 Tbsp soy sauce

1 stale baguette, sliced
(white or wholegrain, 1-inch slices)

1 cored, thinly sliced soft bartlett or anjou pear
(optional)

2-3 cups grated pepper jack cheese or other favorite

3 Tbsp toasted sliced almonds*
for garnishing (optional)

Sliced or whole dried cranberries for garnishing
(optional)

*See Toasting Nuts and Seeds, p. 10.

Vegetarian Chicken Noodle

Busy mothers will be grateful for this easy, kid-friendly soup. It provides mellow, universally appealing flavors that inspire the fussiest eaters to finish their bowl and even ask for seconds.

Procedure

1. Heat 1 tablespoon of the butter or oil in a 4-quart pot over medium-high heat. Add the onion and celery and sauté for a few minutes until the onion begins to brown.

2. Add 9 cups of the water, raise the heat to high, and bring to a boil. Add the pasta, carrot, bouillon cubes or Spike, thyme, and pepper and boil uncovered for 5 minutes. Add the beans, reduce the heat to medium-low, cover, and simmer for another 5 to 7 minutes.

3. Meanwhile, heat the remaining 1 tablespoon butter or oil in a medium skillet over medium-high heat. Add the veggie chicken and pan-fry for 5 to 10 minutes, stirring occasionally, until most sides are golden. Remove from the heat and set aside.

4. Combine the flour and remaining ¼ cup water until a smooth paste is formed. Add this to the soup slowly, stirring constantly. Add the nutritional yeast and parsley (optional). If the soup seems a little thick, add a bit more water. Add salt to taste if needed and simmer for a few more minutes.

5. Remove from the heat, add the veggie chicken to the whole soup or to individual portions, and serve.

> Hands-on prep time: 15 minutes
> Cook time: 20 minutes
> Total time: 35 minutes
> Makes about 10 cups

Ingredients

2 Tbsp butter or oil

½ cup diced onion

1½ cups chopped celery
plus leaves (3 stalks)

9¼ cups water

8 ounces linguine pasta,
broken into 2-inch segments

¾ cup thinly sliced carrot
(1-2 carrots)

3 vegetarian chicken bouillon cubes or 3 Tbsp Spike

½ tsp dried thyme

¼ tsp black pepper

1 cup chopped green beans, fresh or frozen

One 12-ounce package veggie chicken burgers or nuggets, diced*

¼ cup unbleached white flour

3-4 Tbsp nutritional yeast

¼ cup minced Italian parsley
(optional)

Salt to taste

*You can substitute 1½ cups finely cubed firm tofu and use 1 tsp Spike when pan-frying.

Homestyle Minestrone
with Veggie Cream Cheese

Here's an easy soup to please a fussy crowd. It yields a big pot and is popular with both kids and adults. Serve it with warm wholegrain bread and the vegetable cream cheese topping for a cozy lunch or supper.

Procedure

1. Heat the oil in a 6-quart pot over high heat. Add the onion, celery, and garlic and sauté for a few minutes until they begin to brown.

2. Add the remaining ingredients except the broccoli, parsley or basil, and Veggie Cream Cheese. Bring to a boil, reduce the heat to medium, cover, and simmer for about 5 minutes. Add the broccoli and simmer for another 10 minutes. Meanwhile, prepare the Veggie Cream Cheese (optional).

3. Remove from the heat, add the parsley or basil, and stir well. Ladle into bowls, garnish with the Veggie Cream Cheese (optional) or fresh grated parmesan (or both), and serve.

Tips/Variations

Vary the veggies: This is a casual recipe you can play around with. If you've got a zucchini or a small eggplant, feel free to chop it up and toss it in along with the broccoli in Step 2. Also, 1 or 2 cups baby spinach make a fine addition in Step 3.

> **Hands-on prep time:** 20 minutes
> **Cook time:** 25 minutes
> **Total time:** 40 minutes
> **Makes** about 12-14 cups

Ingredients

1 Tbsp oil

1 cup slivered red onion

1 cup chopped celery (2 stalks)

1 Tbsp minced garlic (2-3 cloves)

6 cups water

One 28-ounce can diced tomato

3-ounce chunk parmesan
plus extra grated for garnishing

2½ tsp salt or to taste

1 cup chopped carrot
(1-2 carrots)

¾ cup uncooked small pasta
(like ditalini, shells, orzo, or tubatini)

1½ cups cooked or canned romano, cannellini, or kidney beans*
(rinsed and well drained)

1 Tbsp Italian seasoning

¾ cup frozen corn

⅓ cup tomato paste

1½ tsp sugar

4 cups chopped broccoli
(including peeled stems) (1 bunch)

¼ cup minced Italian parsley or basil

1 recipe Veggie Cream Cheese
for garnishing (p. 299, optional)

*Romano beans are also known as pink beans, and cannellini are also called white beans.

Sopa de Tortilla

This is one of Mexico's most popular soups. Traditionally, it's a simple, full-flavored, tomato-chipotle broth topped with crispy, fried tortilla strips. To boost it up to meal status, include tasty add-ins like garlicky Wilted Spinach and a scoop of Quinoa Pilaf.

The best approach to making Sopa de Tortilla: If making the Quinoa Pilaf (p. 290), put the quinoa on to cook first (it takes just under 20 minutes) and prepare the soup in the meantime. As the quinoa and soup cook, prepare the Tortilla Strips and Wilted Spinach (optional). Because the pilaf can be added warm or room temperature, you can also prepare it in advance.

Procedure

1. Prepare the Quinoa Pilaf. When it's done, set it aside and add it to the soup with the other add-ins later if desired.

2. Heat the oil in a 4-quart pot over medium-high heat. Add the onion and celery and sauté for a few minutes until they begin to brown. Add the tomato, cover, and simmer for a few minutes.

3. Add the remaining ingredients, cover, and bring to a boil. Reduce the heat to medium-low and simmer for 10 to 15 minutes. Meanwhile, prepare the add-ins (see next page).

4. Remove from the heat, ladle into bowls, and serve with add-ins and garnishes of choice (we like all of them and everyone prefers to fix up their own soup).

Tips/Variations

Shortcuts: When pinched for time, make the pilaf with couscous instead of quinoa as it cooks in just a few minutes. You can also eliminate the spinach add-in or simply add the spinach directly to the soup a few minutes before serving.

> Hands-on prep time: 35 minutes
> Cook time: 35 minutes
> Total time: 1 hour 20 minutes (variable)
> Makes 8 cups soup plus add-ins (4-6 servings)

Ingredients

- 1 recipe Quinoa Pilaf (p. 290)
- 1 Tbsp oil
- 1 cup chopped onion
- 1½ cups chopped celery (3 stalks)
- One 28-ounce can diced tomato (or 3½ cups fresh)
- 4 cups water
- 1-2 finely minced canned chipotle peppers* plus 2 tsp adobo sauce
- 1 Tbsp minced fresh oregano leaves or ¼ cup minced cilantro
- 1 tsp ground cumin
- 2 tsp salt or to taste
- 1 Tbsp minced garlic (2-3 cloves)
- 1 Tbsp sugar

*You can also blend the chipotle with 1 cup of the tomato and add this purée to the soup.

Crispy Tortilla Strip Add-In

Ingredients

2-3 Tbsp oil
3 corn tortillas, cut into ¼-inch strips
Sprinkle of salt

Procedure

Heat the oil in a medium skillet over high heat, add the tortilla strips, and fry for a few minutes, stirring occasionally, in batches if necessary and adding a little more oil if needed. When the strips are crispy, place them on several paper towels to drain excess oil. Sprinkle with salt and set aside.

Wilted Spinach Add-In (optional)

Ingredients

1 Tbsp oil
1 tsp minced garlic
3 cups whole baby spinach leaves (packed)
⅛ tsp salt

Procedure

In the same skillet, heat the oil over medium-high heat. Add the garlic and sauté for 30 seconds. Add the spinach and salt and sauté for a few minutes until the spinach is wilted. Set aside.

Additional Garnishes (optional)

Sour cream
Avocado slices
Lemon or lime slices

New England Chowder

A New England clam chowder without clams? Most definitely. Serve it with onion rings or oven-baked sweet potato fries to make a tasty, satisfying meal.

Procedure

1. Melt 2 teaspoons of the butter in a 5-quart pot over medium heat. Add the onion, celery, and garlic and sauté for a few minutes until they begin to brown.

2. Increase the heat to high and add the water, potato, mixed vegetables, bay leaves, thyme, pepper, 1¾ teaspoons of the salt, and 1 tablespoon of the nori. Bring to a boil, reduce the heat to medium, cover, and simmer for 15 minutes or until the potato is tender.

3. Meanwhile, melt the remaining 2 teaspoons butter in a medium skillet over medium heat. Add the mushrooms and sauté for a few minutes until they begin to brown. Add the remaining 1 tablespoon nori to the mushrooms along with the remaining ¼ teaspoon salt. Cook for another 30 seconds, then remove from the heat and set aside.

4. Now, combine the half-and-half with the flour until a smooth paste forms. Add the paste to the soup, stirring constantly to ensure that no lumps form. The soup should thicken immediately. Add the simulated bacon bits and parsley.

5. Once the potato is tender, remove from the heat. Stir in the nori-mushroom mixture. Taste and add more salt if necessary. Ladle into bowls and serve.

Tips/Variations

Canned mushrooms instead of fresh: Several testers used canned mushrooms instead of fresh and said it was unbelievable how much the texture resembled clams. If you use them, simply reduce the mushroom measurement to 1 cup and rinse and drain them well.

Hands-on prep time: 20 minutes
Cook time: 25 minutes
Total time: 40 minutes
Makes about 10 cups

Ingredients

4 tsp butter
1 cup chopped onion
1 cup chopped celery (2 stalks)
2 Tbsp minced garlic (4-6 cloves)
5 cups water
3 cups cubed potato
   (2-3 potatoes)
1 cup frozen mixed vegetables
   (like carrot and corn)
2 bay leaves
½ tsp dried thyme
½ tsp black pepper
2 tsp salt or to taste
2 Tbsp minced nori seaweed*
   or to taste
2 cups chopped button
   mushrooms
1 cup half-and-half (cream)
⅓ cup unbleached white flour
1-2 Tbsp simulated bacon bits
1 tsp dried parsley
   (or 1 Tbsp minced fresh)

*Fold a nori sheet 3 times and mince it with scissors. Nori flakes are also available in a shaker—a tasty Japanese condiment called furikake. You can find furikake in Asian markets and the Asian section of some grocery stores. You can also use any other type of seaweed, such as hijiki or arame. These should be soaked for a few minutes first, then minced.

Hearty Vegetable

When cool weather arrives each autumn, I love to go camping with my family and friends. With big hugs and hearty vegetable chowders, it's easy to stay warm.

Mellow Potato Curry

Beautifully textured and laced with subtle curry spices like cumin, mustard, and cilantro, this mellow and delicious soup is a silken delight for the palate. Though elegant and great for entertaining, it's also agreeable family fare—especially with crispy vegetable samosas and basmati rice.

Procedure

1. Place the water, potato, squash, curry powder, pepper, and 2½ teaspoons of the salt in a 5-quart pot and bring to a boil over high heat. Reduce the heat to medium, cover, and simmer for 10 to 15 minutes until the potato and squash are tender.

2. Meanwhile, heat 2 tablespoons of the ghee or oil over high heat in a medium skillet and add the tofu, leek, and remaining ½ teaspoon salt. Pan-fry for 5 to 10 minutes, stirring occasionally, until the tofu is golden on most sides. Set aside.

3. Remove 2 cups of broth and 2 cups of tender potatoes and squash, place in a blender along with the peanut butter, and blend until smooth. Return to the soup and stir through.

4. Add the tofu and leek to the soup (reserve some of the leek for garnishing if you like). Then, using the same frying pan, heat the remaining 2 tablespoons of ghee or oil over high heat. Add the cumin seeds and sizzle for about 20 to 30 seconds until the seeds turn a dark brown. Then add the mustard seeds and chili flakes and sizzle for another 5 to 10 seconds. Immediately add to the soup. Watch out for sputter!

5. Add the zucchini and cilantro or mint (optional) to the soup, remove from the heat, and let it sit for a couple of minutes to let the zucchini soften slightly. Ladle into bowls, garnish with the reserved leek, and serve.

Hands-on prep time: 20 minutes
Cook time: 30 minutes
Total time: 35 minutes
Makes about 12 cups

Ingredients

- 7 cups water
- 6 cups cubed yukon gold potato (6 potatoes)
- 3 cups cubed butternut or other sweet squash (1½ pounds)
- 1½ tsp madras curry powder
- ¾ tsp black pepper
- 3 tsp salt or to taste
- 4 Tbsp ghee or oil
- 1½ cups finely cubed extra-firm tofu
- 1½ cups finely sliced leek (2 leeks)
- ½ cup unsalted peanut butter
- ½ tsp cumin seeds
- ½ tsp black mustard seeds
- ½ tsp dried chili flakes
- ¼ cup finely diced zucchini
- 2 Tbsp minced cilantro or mint leaves (optional)

Tex-Mex Cauliflower Soup

This rustic Southwestern vegetable soup is easy to throw together for casual everyday fare. It becomes more flavorful the longer it simmers, but since the vegetables begin to lose their form and texture, I don't like to cook it too long, preferring the cauliflower florets whole and tender.

Procedure

1. Heat the oil in a 5-quart pot over high heat. Add the onion and sauté for a few minutes until it begins to brown. Add the celery and garlic and sauté for another minute or so.

2. Add the remaining ingredients and bring to a boil. Reduce the heat to medium, cover, and simmer for 10 to 15 minutes until the cauliflower is tender (or longer if desired). Ladle into bowls and serve.

Tips/Variations

Garnish possibilities: Chopped cilantro, sour cream, grated cheddar or pepper jack cheese, and/or lime wedges.

Serve with Chili Lime Tortilla Crisps (p. 289) and guacamole.

Hands-on prep time: 20 minutes
Cook time: 20 minutes
Total time: 40 minutes
Makes about 8 cups

Ingredients

2 Tbsp oil

1 cup diced onion

⅔ cup diced celery (1-2 stalks)

1 Tbsp minced garlic (2-3 cloves)

1-2 finely minced canned chipotle peppers plus 2 tsp adobo sauce

5 cups water

One 15-ounce can diced tomato (or 1½ cups fresh)

5 cups bite-size cauliflower florets (1 large head)

3 cups diced mixed bell pepper (like yellow, orange, red, and/or green, 2-3 peppers)

1½ cups diced zucchini (1 zucchini)

1½ cups frozen corn

2 bay leaves

2 tsp salt or to taste

2 tsp dried oregano

1 tsp dried cumin

1 tsp sugar

Broccoli Cheddar Soup

Creamy, cheesy, and totally delicious, this recipe is almost guaranteed to convert anyone who doesn't like broccoli. Toasted caraway seeds give this recipe a cozy, homestyle scent that will lure people to your kitchen.

Procedure

1. Heat the oil or butter in a 5-quart pot over medium-high heat. Add the onion, garlic, and caraway seeds and sauté for a few minutes until the onion begins to brown.

2. Add 5 cups of the water and the broccoli, bay leaves, thyme, salt, and pepper. Increase the heat to high and bring to a boil. Then reduce the heat to medium, cover, and simmer for about 5 minutes.

3. Meanwhile, mix the flour with the remaining 1 cup water to form a smooth paste. Add this to the soup gradually, stirring constantly, and simmer 5 minutes more or until the broccoli is tender. Remove from the heat. Remove bay leaves.

4. Place 3 cups soup and the cream cheese in a blender and blend until smooth. Return to the pot. Add the cheddar and stir through until thoroughly melted. Add a little more water or some milk if it seems too thick, and adjust the salt if necessary. Ladle into bowls and serve.

Tips/Variations

Cheese variations: This soup is also delicious made with colby, monterey jack, or pepper jack cheese.

> **Hands-on prep time:** 20 minutes
> **Cook time:** 20 minutes
> **Total time:** 35 minutes
> **Makes** about 11 cups

Ingredients

1 Tbsp oil or butter

1 cup chopped onion

2 Tbsp minced garlic
(4-6 cloves)

¼ tsp caraway seeds

6 cups water

8-9 cups chopped broccoli
(including peeled stems)
(2 bunches)

3 bay leaves

2 tsp dried thyme

1½ tsp salt or to taste

¼ tsp black pepper

3 Tbsp unbleached white flour

One 8-ounce package cream cheese

2 cups grated cheddar cheese
(8 ounces)

Oven-Roasted Vegetable Soup

Here's a rustic and richly flavored soup that makes the most of oven-roasted vegetables. I came up with it one evening when I tossed whatever vegetables I had into a big roasting pan and seasoned them with simple dried spices and balsamic vinegar. When they came out of the oven, caramelized and saturated with flavor, I partially blended them into this easy soup.

Procedure

1. Preheat the oven to 375°F.

2. Place all the ingredients except the water and Braggs or tamari in a large (16 x 11-inch) roasting pan or casserole dish and toss until the veggies are well coated with the seasonings. Roast for 1 hour 15 minutes or until tender and caramelized, turning once.

3. Place ¼ of the roasted veggies in a blender with some of the water so that it reaches the 5-cup mark and blend until smooth. Pour into a 4-quart pot along with the remaining veggies and water and the Braggs or tamari. Bring to a boil over high heat and add a little more water and Braggs or tamari if necessary.

4. Remove from the heat, ladle into bowls, and serve.

Tips/Variations

Garnish possibilities: Dress up your soup with fresh aromatic fennel greens, crumbled feta, or dollops of creamy goat cheese.

Vary the veggies and seasonings: Swap yam for potato, broccoli for cauliflower, carrot for parsnip, or celeriac for celery. Instead of tarragon, you can also season with thyme, rosemary, or Italian seasoning.

Hands-on prep time: 20-30 minutes
Cook time: 1 hour 20 minutes
Total time: 1 hour 45 minutes
Makes about 9 cups

Ingredients

4 cups cubed potato (3-4 potatoes)

4 cups bite-size cauliflower florets

3 cups chopped fennel bulb (2 bulbs)

2 cups chopped red bell pepper (2 peppers)

2 cups chopped parsnip (3 parsnips)

1½ cups chopped celery plus leaves (3-4 stalks)

1 cup chopped onion

5 cloves sliced garlic

¼ cup oil

1 Tbsp dried tarragon

2 tsp salt or to taste

2 tsp paprika

2 tsp ground cumin

2 tsp dried oregano

Fresh-ground black pepper to taste

2-3 Tbsp balsamic vinegar

5-6 cups water

¼ cup Bragg Liquid Aminos or tamari

Young Vegetable Chowder

I love the springtime, when young, tender local vegetables overflow the market stalls. The season's harvest is well celebrated with this delightful vegan cream of vegetable.

Procedure

1. Heat the oil in a 5-quart pot over high heat. Add the onions and sauté for a few minutes until they begin to brown. Add the garlic and brussels sprouts and sauté for a couple of more minutes until the garlic begins to brown.

2. Add the water, carrots, artichoke, Spike, thyme, and Braggs or tamari. Bring to a boil, reduce the heat to medium, cover, and simmer for 10 minutes.

3. Add the potato flakes and corn, stirring constantly. Simmer for another 5 minutes, remove from the heat, and stir in the remaining ingredients. Ladle into bowls and serve.

Tips/Variations

Brussels sprouts variation: If you're not a fan of brussels sprouts, use broccoli or cauliflower instead.

> **Hands-on prep time:** 15 minutes
> **Cook time:** 25 minutes
> **Total time:** 40 minutes
> **Makes** about 9 cups

Ingredients

2 Tbsp oil

1 cup chopped onion

1 dozen pearl onions,* peeled and trimmed

1½ Tbsp minced garlic (3-4 cloves)

4 cups quartered brussels sprouts, ends trimmed

6 cups water

2 cups whole or chopped baby carrots (about 1½ dozen)

1 cup quartered marinated artichoke hearts, lightly rinsed and patted dry

1 Tbsp Spike

1 tsp dried thyme

¼ cup Bragg Liquid Aminos or tamari

1-2 cups dried potato flakes

1 cup frozen corn

¼ cup minced fresh herbs (like parsley, basil, and/or dill)

¼ cup nutritional yeast

2 Tbsp apple cider vinegar

Salt to taste

*You can easily remove the pearl onion skins by blanching them first (see p. 16).

Russian Sweet & Sour

Also known as *schi, this Russian-inspired sweet and sour cabbage soup is a full-flavored, fuss-free homestyle recipe that's super-easy, quick, and inexpensive to make. Tangy, unique, and satisfying, it feels like a special soup despite the everyday ingredients.*

Procedure

1. Heat the butter or oil in a 5-quart pot over medium-high heat. Add the onion and carrot and sauté for a few minutes until they begin to soften. Add the cabbage, potato or turnip, and garlic and sauté for another few minutes until the cabbage softens.

2. Add the tomato, water, Spike, and paprika, increase the heat to high, and bring to a boil. Reduce the heat to medium and add the cranberries, sugar, vinegar, dill, and ginger. Cover and simmer for 10 minutes or until the potato or turnip is tender.

3. Remove from the heat and add salt and pepper to taste if necessary. Ladle into bowls, garnish with sour cream and dill, and serve.

Tips/Variations

Make it a meal: Top or serve with Seasoned TVP Nuggets (p. 293). Complement with pierogies and warm buttered bread.

> Hands-on prep time: 15 minutes
> Cook time: 25 minutes
> Total time: 35 minutes
> Makes about 9 cups

Ingredients

1½ Tbsp butter or oil

1 cup chopped onion

1 cup chopped carrot (1-2 carrots)

4 cups slivered green or savoy cabbage

1½ cups cubed potato or turnip

1½ Tbsp minced garlic (3-4 cloves)

One 15-ounce can diced tomato (or 2 cups fresh)

5½ cups water

2 Tbsp Spike

1 tsp paprika

½ cup minced or whole dried cranberries

3 Tbsp sugar

3 Tbsp apple cider vinegar

1 Tbsp minced fresh dill (or 1 tsp dried) plus extra fresh for garnishing

2 tsp minced ginger

Salt and pepper to taste

Sour cream or Cashew Sour Cream (p. 298) for garnishing

Winter Squash Potato Soup

This quick and tasty recipe is the ultimate everyday soup. It benefits greatly from garden-fresh lemongrass, but if you don't have any of these fragrant stalks growing in your vegetable patch, make sure the ones you buy are not old or dry. Lemongrass releases more flavor when it's fresh and moist.

Procedure

1. Place all the ingredients in a 5-quart pot and bring to a boil over high heat. Boil for 5 minutes, stirring occasionally. Reduce the heat to medium-low, cover, and simmer for 15 to 20 minutes until the potato and squash are tender or partially dissolving.

2. Remove the lemongrass and place 4 cups soup in a blender and blend until smooth. Return to the pot and stir through. Ladle into bowls and serve.

Tips/Variations

Serve with jasmine rice or a quick pad thai stirfry.

Hands-on prep time: 15 minutes
Cook time: 30 minutes
Total time: 40 minutes
Makes about 10 cups

Ingredients

2-4 Tbsp minced ginger or to taste

6 cups chopped butternut or other sweet squash (2½ pounds)

2 cups chopped yukon gold potato (2 potatoes)

One 28-ounce can diced tomato (or 3½ cups fresh)

4 stalks lemongrass, crushed* (use a rolling pin)

One 14-ounce can coconut milk

3 cups water

¼ cup soy sauce

Salt to taste

*See Preparing Lemongrass, p.12.

Hearty Root Vegetable Chowder

Cheesy, creamy, and filled with tender, flavorful root veggies like parsley root, yam, and rutabaga, this easy soup is definitely a winter staple. Serve it with warm, buttery garlic bread for dipping.

Procedure

1. Heat the oil in a 4-quart pot over medium-high heat. Add the onion, garlic, and caraway seeds and sauté for a few minutes until they begin to brown. Add the yam, parsley root or parsnip, celery, and rutabaga or turnip and sauté for another 3 minutes or so, stirring occasionally, until the yam begins to brown slightly.

2. Add the water, Spike, turmeric, sage, and bay leaves, increase the heat to high, and bring to a boil. Reduce the heat to medium, cover, and simmer for 10 to 15 minutes until the vegetables are tender.

3. Remove the bay leaves and place 3 cups of the soup and the cream cheese in a blender, then blend until smooth. Return to the pot and stir through. Ladle into bowls, garnish with fresh-ground pepper, and serve.

Tips/Variations

Fresh herb variations: Add 3 sprigs of fresh lemon thyme when you can find it. A sprig of fresh rosemary or tarragon also adds lovely flavor.

> **Hands-on prep time:** 15 minutes
> **Cook time:** 25 minutes
> **Total time:** 35 minutes
> **Makes** about 8 cups

Ingredients

- 1 Tbsp oil
- 1 cup chopped onion
- 1 Tbsp minced garlic (2-3 cloves)
- ¾ tsp caraway seeds
- 2 cups chopped yam
- 1 cup chopped parsley root or parsnip (2 roots)
- 1 cup chopped celery (1-2 stalks)
- 1 cup diced rutabaga or turnip
- 5 cups water
- 2 Tbsp Spike or to taste
- ¼ tsp turmeric
- ½ tsp dried rubbed sage
- 2 bay leaves
- One 8-ounce package cream cheese
- Fresh-ground black pepper to taste

Albondigas

Brothy, spicy, and fragrant, this vegetarian version of Albondigas (a.k.a. Mexican Meatball Soup) is delicious with chunks of hearty yucca and veggie balls. You can enhance the tomato-chipotle broth with kaffir lime leaves—a touch that really makes it special.

Procedure

1. Place the chipotle, adobo sauce, and 1 cup of the water in a blender and blend until smooth. Set aside.

2. Heat the oil in a 5-quart pot over high heat. Add the onion and sauté for a few minutes until it begins to brown. Add the celery and garlic and sauté for another minute or so.

3. Add the chili purée, remaining 8 cups water, tomato, salt, sugar, cumin, lime leaves (optional), and yucca or potato and bring to a boil. Reduce the heat to medium, cover, and simmer for about 15 minutes or until the yucca or potato is tender. Add the veggie meatballs and cook for another 10 minutes.

4. Ladle the soup into bowls with 3 to 5 meatballs in each, garnish with cilantro and crumbled feta (both optional), and serve.

Tips/Variations

Chipotle shortcut: If you don't feel like pulling out the blender, finely mince the chipotle instead of blending it.

Serve with crusty country-style bread and black olive tapenade or Chili Lime Tortilla Crisps (p. 289). You can also add Crispy Tortilla Strips (p. 42) and serve with Quinoa Pilaf (p. 290).

Hands-on prep time: 20 minutes
Cook time: 35 minutes
Total time: 50 minutes
Makes about 12 cups

Ingredients

1-2 canned chipotle peppers plus 2 tsp adobo sauce

9 cups water

2 Tbsp oil

1 cup slivered onion

2½ cups diced celery (3-4 stalks)

2 Tbsp minced garlic (4-6 cloves)

One 28-ounce can diced tomato (or 3½ cups fresh)

2¾ tsp salt

2 tsp sugar

2 tsp ground cumin

3-4 small kaffir lime leaves* (optional)

1½ cups peeled, cubed yucca or potato

One 12-ounce package vegetarian meatballs** (about 18 balls)

¼ cup minced cilantro for garnishing (optional)

½ cup crumbled feta for garnishing (optional)

*See Kaffir Lime Leaf, p.12.

**Vegetarian meatballs can be found in many grocery and health food stores. I recommend Yves Neatballs.

Cheesy Corn Chipotle Chowder

Everyone loves this soup. Chipotle peppers impart a deep, smoky flavor and some heat, while creamy corn and luscious cheddar provide a rich, full foundation that's truly irresistible.

Procedure

1. Heat the oil in a 5-quart pot over high heat. Add the onion and sauté for a few minutes until it begins to brown. Add the garlic and bell pepper and sauté for a couple of more minutes.

2. Add the water, potato, simulated bacon bits, salt, corn, and oregano, cover, and bring to a boil. Reduce the heat to medium and simmer for another 10 minutes or until the potato is tender. Meanwhile, prepare the garnishes if making them.

3. Ladle 2 cups of the soup into a blender, making sure to get some potato, and blend with the chipotle and adobo sauce until smooth. Return to the pot, stir through, and simmer for another couple of minutes.

4. Add the cheese and stir until thoroughly melted. Add the cream cheese cubes (optional) and stir through. Ladle into bowls, garnish with extra cheese if desired, and serve.

Tips/Variations

Garnish possibilities: For adults, dress it up with sautéed chives and toasted pumpkin seeds. For kids, add a sprinkle of simulated bacon bits and extra grated cheese. You can also swirl a teaspoon of adobo sauce into each bowl.

Serve with: Chili Lime Tortilla Crisps (p. 289) and your favorite salsa.

Hands-on prep time: 15 minutes
Cook time: 25 minutes
Total time: 40 minutes
Makes about 9 cups

Ingredients

1 Tbsp oil

1 cup diced onion

1½ Tbsp minced garlic
(3-4 cloves)

½ cup diced red bell pepper

7 cups water

1½ cups finely cubed potato

2 tsp simulated bacon bits

1¼ tsp salt or to taste

4½ cups corn, fresh or frozen

1½ tsp dried oregano

1-2 canned chipotle peppers
plus 2 tsp adobo sauce

1½ cups grated cheddar cheese
(6 ounces) plus extra for
garnishing if desired

4 ounces cream cheese,
cut into ½-inch cubes (optional)

Mulligatawny

Traditionally a curry-spiced vegetable soup, Mulligatawny has countless variations. Mine draws inspiration from South Indian and Sri Lankan cuisines, using coconut, lemon, and sweet curry spices. The result is a full-flavored, slightly tangy soup that makes the perfect appetizer for any Indian meal.

Procedure

1. Heat the ghee or oil in a 5-quart pot over high heat. Add the onion and garlic and sauté for a few minutes until they begin to brown.

2. Add 5 cups of the water and the lentils, cover, and bring to a boil. Reduce the heat to medium and simmer for about 15 minutes.

3. Add the bell pepper, celery, carrot, tomato, ginger, cinnamon, curry powder, allspice, salt, and sugar. Raise the heat to high and return to a boil. Reduce the heat to medium, cover, and simmer for another 15 minutes or until the lentils are tender. Add the broccoli and corn, raise the heat to high, bring to a boil, and add the coconut, coconut milk, and cilantro.

4. Combine the remaining ¼ cup water with the flour until a smooth paste forms. Add this to the soup gradually, stirring constantly to prevent lumps from forming. Boil another minute, then remove from the heat, ladle into bowls, and serve with slices of lemon.

Tips/Variations

Serve with steamed basmati rice and samosas with Mango Chutney (p. 295).

Vary the veggies: You can also use potato, cauliflower, zucchini, spinach, or whatever you've got in the crisper. A minced fresh chili is also great.

Hands-on prep time: 20 minutes
Cook time: 40 minutes
Total time: 50 minutes
Makes about 8 cups

Ingredients

2 Tbsp ghee or oil

1 cup chopped onion or
   1 dozen pearl onions,*
   peeled and trimmed

1 Tbsp minced garlic (2-3 cloves)

5¼ cups water

½ cup dried brown or green
   lentils, sifted and rinsed well

1½ cups chopped yellow or
   red bell pepper (1-2 peppers)

¾ cup chopped celery (1-2 stalks)

½ cup finely chopped carrot

One 19-ounce can diced
   tomato (or 2 cups fresh)

1 Tbsp minced ginger

1 cinnamon stick or ½ tsp
   ground cinnamon

2 tsp madras curry powder

¼ tsp allspice

2 tsp salt or to taste

1 tsp sugar

2 cups chopped broccoli
   (including peeled stems)

½ cup frozen corn

3 Tbsp desiccated coconut

One 19-ounce can coconut milk

¼ cup minced cilantro

2 Tbsp unbleached white flour

Lemon slices for garnishing

*You can easily remove the pearl onion skins by blanching them first (see p. 16).

Blended

The consistency and flavor of a final blended soup can vary according to the size, quality, and juiciness of your vegetables. Feel free to adjust the water and salt at the end of each recipe to achieve your preferred texture.

Creamy Cashew Soup

This is one of the quickest recipes in this book—and one of the most flavorful. It's also quite rich, so if you're making it as an appetizer, a small bowl will do. If you're cooking for kids, add 3 cups cooked macaroni to make a vegan mac 'n cheese soup.

Procedure

1. Place the water in a kettle or pot and bring to a boil. Meanwhile, place half the cashews with the remaining ingredients (except the croutons) in a blender. Add 3 cups of the boiled water and blend until smooth.

2. Transfer to a 4-quart pot, then blend the remaining cashews with the remaining water until smooth. Transfer to the pot, stir through, and bring the soup to just under a boil over high heat. Remove from the heat, ladle into bowls, garnish with the croutons (optional), and serve.

Tips/Variations

Mayo tip: I don't recommend using Nayonnaise for this recipe as it tends to curdle. I like Follow Your Heart's Vegenaise—it has a fantastic flavor and texture.

Add veggies: Add 2 cups of bite-size broccoli or cauliflower florets or mixed frozen vegetables at Step 2 and simmer over medium heat for an extra 5 to 10 minutes.

Hands-on prep time: 10 minutes
Cook time: 10 minutes
Total time: 15 minutes (not including croutons)
Makes about 8 cups

Ingredients

- **6 cups water**
- **2 cups raw cashews**
- **1 cup nutritional yeast**
- **½ cup eggless mayonnaise**
- **1½-2 Tbsp Spike or to taste**
- **1 tsp granulated garlic**
- **1 tsp mustard powder**
- **2 tsp onion powder**
- **½ tsp turmeric**
- **¼ tsp paprika or cayenne pepper**
- **1 recipe croutons** (p. 288, your choice) for garnishing (optional)

Kabocha Ginger Soup

with Chard Cashew Swirl

This is a very pleasant, simple soup that lets you enjoy the warming energy of sweet winter squash. One of my favorite combinations, kabocha and ginger help increase circulation while strengthening the lungs and immune system. This recipe is the perfect pick-me-up on a chilly autumn day.

Procedure

1. Heat the oil or butter in a 4-quart pot over medium-high heat. Add the ginger, onion, and garlic and sauté for a few minutes until they begin to brown.

2. Add the remaining soup ingredients, increase the heat to high, and bring to a boil. Reduce the heat to medium, cover, and simmer for 10 to 15 minutes until the squash is tender. Meanwhile, prepare the Chard Cashew Swirl (optional).

3. In batches, place the soup in a blender and blend until smooth. Return to the pot and add a bit more salt and sugar if necessary. Ladle into bowls, garnish with the swirl (if using), and serve.

Chard Cashew Swirl (Optional)

Place all the ingredients in a blender and blend until smooth.

Tips/Variations

To peel or not to peel: The dark green skin of kabocha squash will somewhat dim the brilliant orange color of this soup, so if you're going for presentation, you may wish to remove it. Otherwise, leave it on. It's nutritious and doesn't mar the flavor in any way.

> **Hands-on prep time:** 20 minutes
> **Cook time:** 30 minutes
> **Total time:** 40 minutes
> **Makes** about 7 cups

Ingredients

1 Tbsp oil or butter

3 Tbsp minced ginger

1 cup chopped onion

1 Tbsp chopped garlic
   (2-3 cloves)

6-7 cups chopped kabocha
   squash (3 pounds)

4½ cups water

1½ tsp salt or to taste

1 Tbsp sugar or to taste

Chard Cashew Swirl

1 cup lightly steamed swiss
   chard or spinach

½ cup roasted unsalted cashews

¼ cup water

¼ tsp madras curry powder

¼ tsp salt or to taste

Garnet Yam Bisque

with Mango Chutney

This simple soup makes a stunning holiday appetizer. A breeze to prepare, it uses just 6 ingredients to achieve a beautiful silken texture and a delicious full flavor that requires no additional seasoning. The refreshing mango chutney is a must.

Procedure

1. Preheat the oven to 375°F.

2. Prick the yams with a fork and bake for 1 hour 15 minutes or until soft. When the yams are cool enough to handle, peel and chop them. Meanwhile, prepare the chutney.

3. Melt the butter in a 4-quart pot over medium-high heat. Add the ginger and sauté for a minute, then add the yam, sugar, salt, and water. Stir well.

4. In batches, place the ingredients in a blender and blend until smooth. Return to the pot and bring to a quick boil over high heat. Add a little extra water if the soup seems too thick, stir through, and adjust the salt if necessary. Remove from the heat, ladle into bowls, garnish with the chutney, and serve.

> **Hands-on prep time:** 20 minutes
> **Cook time:** 1 hour 25 minutes
> **Total time:** 1 hour 30 minutes
> **Makes** 8-10 cups

Ingredients

5 garnet yams (about 3 pounds)

¼ cup butter

1 Tbsp minced ginger

1-2 Tbsp sugar

1½ tsp salt or to taste

5-6 cups water*

1 recipe Mango Chutney
for garnishing (p. 295)

*Depending on the moisture and size of the yams and the soup consistency you prefer, you may need to add a bit more water.

Wasabi Green Pea Soup

The peppery flavor of wasabi, or Japanese horseradish, subtly permeates this flavorful pea soup, gently stimulating your metabolism and invigorating your lungs. Light yet sustaining, this healthy soup will energize you without making you feel heavy. It's perfect for weight-watchers—though you wouldn't know it upon tasting.

Procedure

1. Place the water and parsnip in a 4-quart pot over high heat and bring to a boil. Reduce the heat to medium-low, cover, and cook for about 10 minutes or until tender.

2. Meanwhile, heat a medium skillet over medium heat, spray with oil spray, and add the tofu cubes. Pan-fry for 5 to 7 minutes, stirring occasionally, until most sides are golden. Add more oil spray when necessary. Add 2 tablespoons of the Braggs or tamari, stir, and cook for another minute or so until dry.

3. Remove the soup from the heat and add the remaining 2 tablespoons Braggs or tamari along with the peas, wasabi, and salt. Allow the peas to blanch for a few minutes.

4. In batches, place the soup in a blender and blend until smooth. Return to the pot, add the tofu, and stir through. Bring to a quick boil over high heat, then remove from the heat, ladle into bowls, and serve.

Tips/Variations

Serve with a side of Slimming Slaw (p. 296) or Summer Salsa (p. 294) for a delightful healthy lunch.

Hands-on prep time: 10 minutes
Cook time: 20 minutes
Total time: 30 minutes
Makes about 8 cups

Ingredients

6 cups water

2 cups chopped parsnip
(3-4 parsnips)

Oil spray

1 cup firm tofu,
cut into ¼-inch cubes

4 Tbsp Bragg Liquid Aminos or tamari

4¼ cups frozen peas
(thawed, 20 ounces)

2 tsp wasabi powder or paste or to taste

1 tsp salt or to taste

Roasted Tomato Herb Soup
with Fresh Dill Cream

If you're lucky enough to have big, juicy tomatoes growing in your garden, this recipe will make excellent use of them. If you're not so fortunate, keep in mind that ripe, quality tomatoes are essential for this soup, so it's worth the splurge to get the best you can. Try using sweet, low-acid heirlooms if you find them at the farmers' market.

Procedure

1. Preheat the oven to 400°F.

2. Place the tomatoes, onion, and garlic cloves in a large roasting pan, rub them with the oil, sprinkle with the Italian seasoning, and bake for 15 to 20 minutes until the tomatoes are juicy and wilted. Meanwhile, prepare the Fresh Dill Cream.

3. In batches, place the roasted tomatoes, onion, and garlic (and any juices) in a blender along with the fresh herbs and water, silken tofu, or half-and-half and blend until smooth.

4. Pour the blended soup into a 4-quart pot, add the Braggs and sugar, and stir through. Add a little more water if you need to and add salt and pepper to taste. Place the pot over high heat, bring to a boil, and remove from the heat. Ladle into bowls, garnish with the Fresh Dill Cream, and serve.

Tips/Variations

Serve as a beautiful appetizer with an assortment of Pita Crisps (p. 289).

Garnish alternatives: You can also garnish with small dollops of goat cheese or plain sour cream or with tiny cubes of cream cheese. A drizzle of herb-infused olive oil is also lovely.

> Hands-on prep time: 15 minutes
> Cook time: 25 minutes
> Total time: 35 minutes
> Makes about 8 cups

Ingredients

8-10 large tomatoes, quartered
½ cup thinly sliced onion
2 cloves garlic
2 Tbsp oil
1 Tbsp Italian seasoning
½ cup chopped Italian parsley and/or basil
1 cup water, silken tofu, or half-and-half (cream)
3 Tbsp Bragg Liquid Aminos
2 tsp sugar
Salt and pepper to taste
1 recipe Fresh Dill Cream for garnishing (p. 298)

Roasted Fennel Carrot Blend

Simple, flavorful, and healthy, this palate-cleansing soup is the perfect appetizer because it won't spoil your appetite. Fennel is also a natural digestive aid that makes it easier for your body to assimilate vital nutrients.

Procedure

1. Preheat the oven to 400°F.

2. Spread the fennel, onion, and zucchini separately on a large baking tray, drizzle with the oil, and sprinkle with ½ teaspoon of the salt and the fennel seeds. Bake for 20 to 25 minutes, tossing once halfway.

3. Meanwhile, place the water or broth, bouillon cube(s) (if using water), and carrot in a 4-quart pot and bring to a boil over high heat. Reduce the heat to medium, cover, and simmer for 10 to 15 minutes until the carrots are tender.

4. In batches, place the carrots, broth, half of the fennel, and all of the onion in a blender and blend until smooth, adding a bit more water if necessary. Return to the pot.

5. Add the remaining roasted vegetables and remaining teaspoon salt, add pepper to taste, and stir through. Raise the heat to high and gently bring to a boil. Remove from the heat and serve.

Tips/Variations

Carrot tip: Test your carrots first to make sure they're sweet. If they're a little on the dull side, you may want to add some honey or sugar to taste.

Serve as a prelude to a variety of meals—from lasagna to veggie burgers. You can also serve as a light lunch with your favorite focaccia.

Hands-on prep time: 20 minutes
Cook time: 40 minutes
Total time: 40 minutes
Makes about 8 cups

Ingredients

4 cups chopped fennel bulb
(2 bulbs)

½ cup chopped vidalia or other sweet onion

2 cups chopped zucchini
(1 large zucchini)

2 Tbsp oil

1½ tsp salt or to taste

¾ tsp fennel seeds

6 cups water or Basic Veggie Broth (p. 282)

1-2 veggie bouillon cubes
(only if using water)

6 cups roughly chopped carrot
(8-10 carrots)

Fresh-ground black pepper to taste

Roasted Celeriac Parsnip Soup
with Herb-Infused Oil

Subtle, soft, and slightly nutty, this recipe is an excellent showcase for roasted celeriac and parsnip. Both make great blended soups because they lend natural creaminess without being fattening. Serve as an appetizer or accompaniment to a variety of dishes—from a colorful Greek salad to savory cabbage rolls.

Procedure

1. Preheat the oven to 400°F.

2. Spread the celeriac, parsnip, garlic, celery, and onion or shallot in a baking pan. Drizzle with the oil, sprinkle with the salt, and toss well. Bake for about 45 minutes, turning once halfway, until the veggies are tender and slightly caramelized.

3. Place the roasted veggies, water, bay leaves, peppercorns, and tarragon in a 5-quart pot over high heat and bring to a boil. Reduce the heat to medium, cover, and simmer for 10 to 15 minutes. Add the lemon zest and nutmeg, stir well, and remove from the heat.

4. Remove the bay leaves and place 4 cups of the soup in a blender and blend until smooth. Return to the pot and stir through. Ladle into bowls, garnish with the Herb-Infused Oil or chives or parsley, and serve.

Tips/Variations

Potato variation: If you haven't any celeriac on hand, substitute potato for a simple, nourishing alternative. Stir in a cup of grated sharp white cheddar if you like.

> **Hands-on prep time:** 20 minutes
> **Cook time:** 1 hour 10 minutes
> **Total time:** 1 hour 15 minutes
> **Makes** about 8 cups

Ingredients

4 cups cubed celeriac*
(1 medium-large root)

3 cups chopped parsnip
(4-6 parsnips)

2 Tbsp minced garlic (4-6 cloves)

1 cup chopped celery (2 stalks)

¼ cup sliced onion or shallot
(about 3 shallots)

2 Tbsp oil

2 tsp salt

8 cups water

2 bay leaves

¼ tsp whole black peppercorns

1½ tsp dried tarragon

½ tsp finely minced or grated lemon zest

Dash of nutmeg

Herb-Infused Oil (p. 297) **or minced chives or parsley**
for garnishing

*See Peeling Celeriac, p. 13.

Easy Zucchini Bisque
with Apple Radish Salsa

Light, fresh, simple, and summery, this is the ultimate last-minute soup. Kids love it too, though I usually serve it to them with croutons rather than the salsa. This soup can also be served chilled, making it perfect for lunch the next day.

Procedure

1. Heat the butter or oil in a 4-quart pot over medium-high heat. Add the zucchini, tarragon, and salt and sauté for a few minutes until slightly golden. Add the water, raise the heat to high, cover, and bring to a boil. Boil for about 5 minutes or until the zucchini is tender. Meanwhile, prepare the salsa if making.

2. In batches, place the zucchini, cooking water, and cream cheese in a blender and blend until smooth. Return to the pot and simmer uncovered on the lowest heat while you finish preparing the salsa.

3. Ladle the soup into bowls and garnish with the paprika and Apple Radish Salsa (optional).

> **Hands-on prep time:** 15 minutes
> **Cook time:** 20 minutes
> **Total time:** 30 minutes (not including salsa)
> **Makes** about 8 cups

Ingredients

1 Tbsp butter or oil

10 cups chopped zucchini
(5-6 zucchinis)

1½ Tbsp minced fresh tarragon (or 2 tsp dried)

1¼ tsp salt or to taste

5 cups water

One 8-ounce package cream cheese

Sprinkling of paprika
for garnishing

1 recipe Apple Radish Salsa
for garnishing (p. 294, optional)

Italian Summer Squash Soup

This soup makes a delectable summertime appetizer. It turns out a little differently each time I make it depending on the quality and juiciness of the vegetables. I like to use sunburst patty pans because of their vibrant yellow color, but really any summer squash will do—scallopini, crookneck, etc.

Procedure

1. Preheat the oven to 400°F.

2. Spread the tomato, zucchini, patty pan, onion, and garlic on a large baking pan and drizzle with the oil. Sprinkle with the Italian seasoning and toss the veggies well. Bake for about 20 minutes or until tender and juicy, turning once after 10 minutes.

3. In batches, place in a blender the water, salt, pepper, sugar, all of the tomato and tomato juice, both cloves of garlic, and ¾ of the remaining roasted veggies and blend until smooth.

4. Transfer the mixture to a 4-quart pot and add the remaining roasted veggies. Simmer over medium-high heat for a few minutes and add a little water if it seems too thick, adjusting the salt if necessary. Stir in the parsley or basil. Ladle into bowls, garnish with extra herbs, and serve.

Tips/Variations

Mushroom variation: Roast a large chopped portobello mushroom with the veggies. Don't include it in the blended portion, but add it to the puréed soup along with the other reserved veggies.

Make it a meal: Top or serve with Smoky Tempeh (p. 291). Complement with a tangy mesclun salad topped with shaved asiago and toasted hazelnuts.

> Hands-on prep time: 15 minutes
> Cook time: 25 minutes
> Total time: 40 minutes
> Makes about 6 to 8 cups

Ingredients

4 large juicy tomatoes, halved

4-5 cups chopped zucchini (3 zucchinis)

2 cups quartered patty pan squash (a.k.a. flying saucers)

1 cup slivered onion

2 whole cloves garlic

2 Tbsp oil

1 Tbsp Italian seasoning

2-3 cups water

1½ tsp salt or to taste

Fresh-ground black pepper to taste

1 Tbsp sugar

¼ cup minced Italian parsley or basil plus extra for garnishing

Beans & Grains

Soups are a great showcase for energizing beans and grains.
A savory broth and tender veggies keep it light, while a
fiber-rich bean or grain lets a soup be hearty, satisfying, and
even meal-caliber without weighing you down.

Wheatberry Florentine

This soup is a delicious way to bring the health-giving wheatberry into your diet. Strengthening and calming, wheatberries promote muscle development and increase your energy. For a less chewy grain, you can use pearl barley instead. The tempeh topping is always a hit, so you may want to make double.

Plan ahead: Soak the wheatberries for 8 to 12 hours prior to cooking. Rinse and drain before adding to the soup. (If using pearl barley, there's no need to soak it.)

Procedure

1. Heat the oil in a 5-quart pot over medium-high heat. Add the onion and garlic and sauté for a few minutes until they begin to brown.

2. Add the wheatberries or barley, water or broth, bouillon cubes (if using water), parmesan, savory, thyme, and salt. Cover, bring to a boil, reduce the heat to medium, and simmer for an hour (if using pearl barley, 45 minutes will do) or until the grains are just tender. Add a bit more water if you need to and adjust the salt accordingly.

3. Add the bell pepper, increase the heat to high, and return to a boil. Add the spinach and artichoke, reduce the heat to medium, and simmer for another 10 minutes. Meanwhile, prepare the tempeh.

4. Remove from the heat, ladle into bowls, garnish with the tempeh and your cheese of choice (optional), and serve.

> **Hands-on prep time:** 20 minutes
> **Cook time:** 1 hour 5 minutes
> **Total time:** 1 hour 20 minutes
> **Makes** about 9 cups

Ingredients

- 1 Tbsp oil
- 1½ cups chopped red onion
- 4 cloves garlic, thinly sliced
- ¾ cup pre-soaked hard red wheatberries or pearl barley
- 9 cups water or Basic Veggie Broth (p. 282)
- 2 veggie bouillon cubes (only if using water)
- One 4-ounce chunk parmesan cheese
- 1 sprig fresh summer savory (or 1 tsp dried)
- 3 sprigs fresh thyme or lemon thyme (or 1 tsp dried)
- 2 tsp salt or to taste
- 1½ cups diced red bell pepper
- 8 cups chopped spinach (1 pound, tightly packed)
- ¾ cup quartered marinated artichoke hearts, lightly rinsed
- 1 recipe Smoky Tempeh (p. 291)
- Crumbled feta, grated parmesan, or creamy goat cheese for garnishing (optional)

Hearty Fall Lentil Soup

Delicious and dependable, this cold-weather favorite is easy to get going on the stovetop when you arrive home from a busy day. It's filled with energizing lentils, sweet nuggets of yam and parsnip, and wholesome flavors that appeal to tastebuds of all ages.

Procedure

1. Heat the oil in a 5-quart pot over high heat. Add the onion and sauté for a few minutes until it begins to brown. Add the garlic and celery and sauté for another minute or two.

2. Add the water, tomato, lentils, sugar, pepper, bay leaves, and sage. Bring to a boil, reduce the heat to medium, cover, and simmer for 20 minutes.

3. Add the yam, parsnip, vinegar, bouillon cube(s), and salt. Increase the heat to high and bring to a boil. Reduce the heat to medium, cover, and simmer for another 20 minutes or until the lentils, yam, and parsnip are tender. Remove from the heat, ladle into bowls, and serve.

Tips/Variations

Make it a meal: Add 1 to 2 cups chopped veggie sausages at the beginning of Step 3, or pan-fry them first in 1 tablespoon oil in a medium skillet over medium-high heat for 5 minutes, stirring occasionally, until golden, then add them to the soup just before serving. Serve with your favorite bread, slathered with butter.

Hands-on prep time: 10 minutes
Cook time: 50 minutes
Total time: 55 minutes
Makes about 10 cups

Ingredients

1 Tbsp oil

1 cup slivered onion

2 Tbsp minced garlic (4-6 cloves)

1 cup chopped celery (2 stalks)

6 cups water

One 28-ounce can diced tomato

1½ cups dried green or brown
   lentils, sifted and rinsed well

2 tsp sugar

½ tsp black pepper

2 bay leaves

½ tsp dried rubbed sage

2 cups chopped yam (1 large yam)

2 cups chopped parsnip
   (3-4 parsnips)

1-2 Tbsp red wine vinegar
   or sherry vinegar

1-2 veggie bouillon cubes

2 tsp salt or to taste

Everyday Bean Chowder

Simple and nutritious, this is one of my favorite "feel better" soups—one I often make when someone isn't feeling 100%. Like many soups and stews, this mellow, comforting recipe tastes even better after a day or two, becoming creamier and more flavorful with time.

Procedure

Place all the ingredients except the yeast and vinegar in a 5-quart pot and bring to a boil over high heat. Reduce the heat to medium-low, cover, and simmer for 1 hour. Add the yeast and vinegar and stir through. Add a little more salt if necessary. Ladle into bowls and serve.

Tips/Variations

Make it a meal: Add 1½ cups cubed firm tofu, or serve with Seasoned TVP Nuggets (p. 293) as a topping or on the side.

Mexican variation: Add 1½ teaspoons chili powder and ¼ cup minced cilantro. A tablespoon of simulated bacon bits will also give the soup a nice smoky flavor.

> **Hands-on prep time:** 20 minutes
> **Cook time:** 1 hour 10 minutes
> **Total time:** 1 hour 30 minutes
> **Makes** about 8 cups

Ingredients

- 5 cups water or Basic Veggie Broth (p. 282)
- 2 cups chopped potato (2 potatoes)
- ½ cup chopped carrot
- ½ cup chopped celery
- ½ cup chopped green beans, fresh or frozen
- 3 Tbsp minced ginger
- 2 cups chopped baby bok choy, spinach, or swiss chard
- One 28-ounce can diced tomato (or 3½ cups fresh)
- 1½ cups cooked or canned pinto beans (rinsed and drained)
- 2 tsp salt or to taste
- 2 Tbsp nutritional yeast
- 1 Tbsp apple cider vinegar

Caribbean Yucca Bean Chowder

This colorful, enlivening chowder is great for both summer and winter. The lime and cilantro impart light, refreshing flavors, while hearty yucca and rich coconut make it substantial and satisfying.

Procedure

1. Heat the oil in a 5-quart pot over medium-high heat. Add the onion and bell pepper and sauté for a few minutes until the onion begins to brown.

2. Add the water or broth, yucca, tomato, beans, coconut milk, desiccated coconut, and salt. Increase the heat to high, bring to a boil, reduce the heat to medium, cover, and simmer for 15 minutes.

3. Add the zucchini and simmer for another 5 minutes or until the yucca is completely tender. Remove from the heat, add the lime juice, cilantro (optional), and chili (optional), and stir through. Ladle into bowls, garnish with plantain chips (optional), and serve.

Tips/Variations

Make it a meal: Top or serve with Smoky Tempeh (p. 291) for a healthy, festive meal. A side dish of spicy baked plantain or yam spears is also great.

> **Hands-on prep time:** 20 minutes
> **Cook time:** 30 minutes
> **Total time:** 40 minutes
> **Makes** about 10 cups

Ingredients

- **1 Tbsp oil**
- **1 cup chopped red onion**
- **1 cup chopped bell pepper** (orange, yellow, or red)
- **5 cups water or Basic Veggie Broth** (p. 282)
- **3 cups peeled, chopped yucca*** (about 1¼ pounds)
- **One 19-ounce can diced tomato** (or 2 cups fresh)
- **1 cup cooked or canned kidney beans** (rinsed and drained)
- **One 14-ounce can coconut milk**
- **3 Tbsp unsweetened desiccated coconut**
- **2½ tsp salt or to taste**
- **1½ cups chopped zucchini**
- **¼ cup lime juice**
- **¾ cup chopped cilantro** (tightly packed, optional)
- **½ tsp minced fresh chili or red chili flakes** (optional)
- **Plantain chips** for garnishing (store-bought, optional)

*See p. 16, What Is Yucca?

Moroccan Chickpea Chowder

with Minted Couscous

My friend Diana has a knack for simple one-dish meals that offer a variety of pleasing textures, colors, and flavors. This recipe is a prime example. The smooth tomato broth is fragrant with sweet, mellow curry spices, while the minted couscous with luscious medjool dates creates a beautiful centerpiece. When making it as an appetizer, serve it without the couscous.

Procedure

1. Heat the oil in a 5-quart pot over medium-high heat. Add the chili, cumin, coriander, garam masala, turmeric, and cinnamon and sizzle for 30 seconds. Add the onion and garlic and sauté for a few minutes until they begin to brown.

2. Add the remaining ingredients except the couscous, increase the heat to high, and bring to a boil. Reduce the heat to medium-low, cover, and simmer for 30 minutes. Meanwhile, prepare the couscous if making.

3. Remove from the heat. Ladle into shallow bowls, place a scoop of the couscous in the center of each portion (optional), and serve.

> **Hands-on prep time:** 25 minutes
> **Cook time:** 40 minutes
> **Total time:** 55 minutes
> **Makes** about 10 cups

Ingredients

1 Tbsp oil

½ tsp red chili flakes

½ tsp ground cumin

½ tsp ground coriander

½ tsp garam masala

½ tsp turmeric

Pinch of cinnamon

1½ cups diced red onion

1 Tbsp minced garlic (2-3 cloves)

3½ cups water

One 28-ounce can puréed tomato (or 3½ cups fresh)

2 cups cooked or canned chickpeas (rinsed and drained)

1 cup diced thin-skinned potato

1 cup diced carrot (1-2 carrots)

1 cup diced red bell pepper

1 cup diced zucchini

1 cup diced celery (2 stalks)

2 cups bite-size cauliflower florets

2¼ tsp salt or to taste

1 Tbsp sugar

1 recipe Minted Couscous (p. 291, optional)

Fiesta Black Bean Soup
with Summer Salsa

Elegant and attractive, rich yet refreshing, this is not your typical black bean soup. The secret ingredient is chocolate, which imparts a rich, subtly sweet flavor. The delicious Summer Salsa provides a lovely contrast in both color and texture; it's the perfect crowning jewel.

Procedure

1. Heat the oil in a 4-quart pot over high heat. Add the onion and garlic and sauté for a few minutes until they begin to brown. Add the cumin, coriander, oregano, and paprika or cayenne and sauté for another 30 seconds.

2. Add the water, beans, and salt. Bring to a boil, reduce the heat to medium-low, cover, and simmer for about 10 minutes while you prepare the salsa.

3. Remove from the heat. In batches, place 5 cups of the soup and the sour cream, lime juice, cilantro (optional), and chocolate in a blender and blend until smooth.

4. Return to the pot, stir, and add a little more water if it seems too thick, adjusting the salt if necessary. Bring to a quick boil and remove from the heat. Ladle into bowls, garnish with the salsa, and serve.

Tips/Variations

Garnish variations: You can also garnish with Avocado Mousse (p. 299), sour cream, minced chives, and/or store-bought salsa.

> **Hands-on prep time:** 20 minutes
> **Cook time:** 20 minutes
> **Total time:** 30 minutes
> **Makes** about 8 cups

Ingredients

2 Tbsp oil

1 cup chopped vidalia or other sweet onion

1½ Tbsp minced garlic (3-4 cloves)

2 tsp ground cumin

1 Tbsp ground coriander

2 tsp dried oregano

1 tsp paprika or ¼ tsp cayenne

3 cups water

4½ cups cooked or canned black beans (rinsed and drained)

1½ tsp salt or to taste (depends on saltiness of beans)

1 cup sour cream

2 Tbsp lime juice

½ cup cilantro (tightly packed) (optional)

¼ cup semisweet or milk chocolate chips or 1 Tbsp cocoa powder

1 recipe Summer Salsa for garnishing (p. 294)

Mighty Mushroom Barley Soup

Everything you need for a wintertime pick-me-up is right here in this tasty, nourishing soup. Barley strengthens the blood and digestive system, while rosemary improves circulation and helps you feel calm, clear-headed, and alert. Protein-rich mushrooms absorb toxins and escort them out of the body.

Procedure

1. Heat 2 tablespoons of the oil in a 5-quart pot over medium-high heat. Add the onion, leek, garlic, mushrooms, and 1 teaspoon of the salt and sauté for a few minutes until the vegetables begin to brown.

2. Add 10½ cups of the water or broth along with the barley, rosemary, pepper, and Braggs or tamari. Increase the heat to high and bring to a boil. Reduce the heat to medium, cover, and simmer for 45 to 60 minutes until the barley is cooked.

3. Meanwhile, heat the remaining tablespoon of oil in a medium skillet over high heat. Add the tofu with the remaining ¼ teaspoon salt and pan-fry for 5 to 7 minutes, stirring occasionally, until the tofu is golden on most sides. When the barley is cooked, add the tofu to the soup.

4. Combine the flour with the remaining ½ cup water or broth until a smooth paste forms. Add this to the soup, stirring constantly to make sure no lumps form. Increase the heat to high and bring to a boil. Remove from the heat, add a little more salt to taste if necessary, ladle into bowls, and serve.

Tips/Variations

"Beef" & Barley variation: Replace the tofu with chopped seitan or diced Boca Burgers (found frozen in most health food and grocery stores) for a vegetarian "Beef" & Barley Soup.

> Hands-on prep time: 20 minutes
> Cook time: 1 hour 20 minutes
> Total time: 1 hour 25 minutes
> Makes about 8 cups

Ingredients

3 Tbsp oil

½ cup chopped onion

1 cup sliced leek (1-2 leeks)

2 Tbsp minced garlic (4-6 cloves)

3½ cups sliced mushrooms

1¼ tsp salt or to taste

11 cups water or Mushroom Broth (p. 283)

¾ cup pearl barley

1 large sprig fresh rosemary (or 1 tsp dried)

¼ tsp black pepper

¼ cup Bragg Liquid Aminos or tamari

2 cups finely cubed extra-firm tofu

½ cup unbleached white flour

Lemony Lentil Chard Soup

You'll feel good about making this Middle Eastern-inspired soup for your family. Tangy, unique, and healthy, it's perfect for casual, everyday dining.

Procedure

1. Place the water or broth and lentils in a 5-quart pot and bring to a boil over high heat. Reduce the heat to medium, cover, and simmer for 45 minutes or until the lentils are tender.

2. Meanwhile, heat the oil in a large skillet over medium-high heat. Add the leek and sauté for a few minutes until it begins to brown. Add the eggplant and ½ teaspoon of the salt and sauté for a few minutes until the eggplant softens. Add the tomato and cook for a few more minutes until the vegetables become saucy.

3. Once the lentils are just tender, add to the pot the saucy veggies, remaining 2 teaspoons salt, chard or spinach, zaatar, paprika, cumin, bouillon cubes (if using water), and zest and simmer for another 10 minutes. Stir in the lemon juice and garlic, ladle into bowls, garnish with lemon slices, and serve.

Tips/Variations

Eggplant variation: If you're not an eggplant fan, use potato and/or zucchini instead.

Zaatar: A common Lebanese seasoning, zaatar can be found in most Middle Eastern grocery shops. Make your own zaatar in whatever quantity you like with equal parts oregano, thyme, toasted sesame seeds, sumac powder, and salt.

Serve with Savory Pita Crisps (p. 289), falafel balls, hummus, and tabouleh.

Hands-on prep time: 15 minutes
Cook time: 1 hour 5 minutes
Total time: 1 hour 5 minutes
Makes about 10 cups

Ingredients

6-7 cups **water** or **Basic Veggie Broth** (p. 282)

1½ cups **brown or green lentils,** sifted and rinsed well

2 Tbsp **oil**

1½ cups **sliced leek** (2 leeks)

4 cups **cubed eggplant** (1 medium eggplant)*

2½ tsp **salt** or to taste

One 19-ounce can **diced tomato** (or 2¼ cups fresh)

4 cups **chopped swiss chard or spinach** (tightly packed)

2½ Tbsp **zaatar**

2 tsp **paprika**

1 Tbsp **ground cumin**

2 **veggie bouillon cubes** (only if using water)

2 Tbsp **grated lemon zest** (zest of 1-2 lemons)

⅓ cup **lemon juice**

1 Tbsp **minced garlic** (2-3 cloves)

Lemon slices for garnishing

*You may wish to salt the eggplant before tossing it in the pot (see p. 13 for method). Test it first to see if it's bitter.

Tuscan Orzo Soup

Whole cloves of mellowed oven-roasted garlic infuse a sumptuous broth filled with tender vegetables, white beans, and orzo pasta. Topped with peppery arugula, toasted hazelnuts, and shaved Asiago, this beautiful, elegant soup is perfect for entertaining.

Plan ahead: This recipe calls for 2 bulbs of roasted garlic (see p. 11 for easy method), which can be made in advance. You'll also need Italian Broth (p. 281).

Procedure

1. Heat the oil in a 5-quart pot over medium-high heat. Add the onion and sauté for a couple of minutes until it begins to brown. Add the celery and mushrooms and sauté for a few more minutes until they begin to brown.

2. Add the tomato, broth, carrot, potato, beans, salt, Italian seasoning, and orzo and bring to a boil. Squeeze the garlic bulbs to pop the buttery cloves out of their skins and into the soup. Add the zucchini, reduce the heat to medium, and simmer for about 10 minutes or until the orzo is cooked.

3. Add the sugar and the arugula or spinach and stir through. Remove from the heat. Ladle into bowls, garnish with Asiago or parmesan, arugula or spinach, and hazelnuts (all optional but delicious), and serve.

Tips/Variations

Broth variation: In place of Italian Broth, use an equal amount of water along with 2 veggie bouillon cubes, 2 tablespoons grated parmesan cheese, 1 to 2 tablespoons tomato paste, and a handful of fresh basil leaves.

Make it a meal: Top or serve with Smoky Tempeh (p. 291).

Hands-on prep time: 25 minutes
Cook time: 25 minutes (not including garlic roasting or Italian Broth time)
Total time: 45 minutes
Makes about 10 cups

Ingredients

- 1 Tbsp oil
- 1 cup slivered red onion
- 1 cup chopped celery (2 stalks)
- 1 cup quartered cremini or button mushrooms
- 1 cup diced tomato
- 7 cups Italian Broth (p. 281)
- ⅔ cup chopped carrot (1-2 carrots)
- 1 cup chopped potato
- 1 cup cooked or canned cannellini beans (a.k.a. white beans, rinsed and drained)
- 1 tsp salt or to taste
- 1 Tbsp Italian seasoning
- ⅔ cup dried orzo pasta
- 2 bulbs roasted garlic (p. 11)
- ⅔ cup diced zucchini
- 1 tsp sugar
- 3 cups baby arugula or spinach (gently packed) plus extra for garnishing (optional)
- Shaved asiago or parmesan cheese for garnishing (optional)
- ¼ cup chopped hazelnuts, toasted and unsalted for garnishing (optional)

Easy Dhal

When spiced to perfection, a mellow, saucy dhal is seen in Ayurveda as one of the most body-balancing, nurturing, and sustaining foods of all. It is highly digestible, gentle on the body, and can be eaten by young children and elderly people alike. In India, dhal is traditionally eaten with rice and chapatis as a light, energizing meal. Try making this delightful dhal for those you love.

Procedure

1. Place the lentils, water, tomato, ginger, and turmeric in a 4-quart pot over high heat. Bring to a boil, reduce the heat to medium, cover, and simmer for about 30 minutes.

2. When the lentils have broken down and the soup is quite smooth, heat the oil or ghee in a small skillet over high heat. Add the cumin and mustard seeds and sauté for a few seconds. When the cumin darkens, add the chili and coriander and stir for a few seconds. Remove from the heat and add immediately to the soup along with the salt.

3. Add the cilantro or mint and garlic and stir through. Ladle into bowls, garnish with extra cilantro or mint, and serve.

Tips/Variations

Veggie variation: Include 1 to 2 cups chopped yam from the very beginning. Or, after the lentils have cooked for about 20 minutes, add 2 cups chopped vegetables, like broccoli, cauliflower, or spinach. Increase the water and salt if necessary.

Coconut variation: Add 1 cup coconut milk a few minutes before serving and increase the salt slightly if necessary.

> **Hands-on prep time:** 10 minutes
> **Cook time:** 40 minutes
> **Total time:** 45 minutes
> **Makes** about 9 cups

Ingredients

2½ cups dried red lentils, sifted and rinsed well

7 cups water

One 15-ounce can diced tomato (or 2 cups fresh)

1½ Tbsp minced ginger

¼ tsp turmeric

1 tsp oil or ghee

1 tsp cumin seeds

1 tsp black mustard seeds

¼ tsp minced fresh chili or red chili flakes

1 tsp ground coriander

2¼ tsp salt or to taste

½ cup minced cilantro or mint leaves plus extra for garnishing

½ Tbsp minced garlic (1-2 cloves)

Pasta e Fagioli

Pasta e Fagioli has been an Italian favorite for centuries and is the epitome of rustic elegance. A casual one-dish meal that everyone loves, this easy pasta and bean soup has often been a saving grace for last-minute dinners.

Procedure

1. Heat the oil in a 5-quart pot over high heat. Add the leek and garlic and sauté for a few minutes until they begin to brown. Add the tomato and basil and cook for a few more minutes until the tomato begins to break down and become saucy.

2. Add the water or broth, beans, salt, and sugar and bring to a boil. Reduce the heat to medium, cover, and simmer for about 10 minutes.

3. Increase the heat to high, return to a boil, and add the pasta. Cook for 8 to 10 minutes until the pasta is tender, then remove from the heat. Ladle into bowls, garnish with pepper, parmesan, and basil, and serve.

Tips/Variations

Vary the herbs, beans, or pasta: Instead of or in addition to basil, feel free to use arugula or Italian parsley. Also, you can use different beans, like romano or borlotti, as well as other pasta shapes, such as orzo or ditalini.

Garnish possibilities: Toasted pine nuts or hazelnuts.

Hands-on prep time: 15 minutes
Cook time: 30 minutes
Total time: 35 minutes
Makes about 10 cups

Ingredients

¼ cup oil

1 cup finely sliced leek (1-2 leeks)

1½ Tbsp minced garlic (3-4 cloves)

One 28-ounce can diced tomato (or 3½ cups fresh)

4 cups roughly chopped basil (gently packed) plus extra for garnishing

4 cups water or Italian Broth (p. 281)

1½ cups cooked or canned cannellini beans (a.k.a. white beans, rinsed and drained)

2 tsp salt or to taste

2 tsp sugar

1 cup dried small pasta shells

Fresh-ground black pepper to taste for garnishing

Parmesan cheese for garnishing

Winter Mushroom Alfredo

Just say the word "alfredo" and immediately you have a captive audience. Rich, mushroomy, and parmesan cheesy, this luscious tarragon-infused cream soup is a spin on fettuccine alfredo. Everyone loves it, especially men and boys.

Procedure

1. Cook the fettuccine according to the package directions, rinse well under cold water, and set aside.

2. Meanwhile, heat 1 tablespoon of the butter or oil in a 5-quart pot over medium-high heat. Add the onion, mushrooms, and garlic and sauté for a few minutes until they begin to brown.

3. Stir the flour into the water until smooth. Add this to the pot along with 1½ teaspoons of the salt and the parmesan, broccoli, asparagus, lima beans (optional), sherry (optional), pepper, and tarragon. Bring to a boil, then reduce the heat to medium-low. Add the half-and-half, cover, and simmer for 10 minutes.

4. Meanwhile, if including the tofu, heat the remaining tablespoon of butter or oil in a medium skillet over medium-high heat. Add the tofu and remaining ¼ teaspoon salt and pan-fry for 5 to 7 minutes, stirring occasionally, until golden on most sides. Set aside.

5. Add the tofu (optional), spinach, and fettuccine to the pot. Add a little more water or half-and-half if necessary and adjust the salt accordingly. Increase the heat to high and gently bring to just under a boil, then remove from the heat. Remove the tarragon sprigs, ladle into bowls, garnish with grated parmesan, and serve.

Tips/Variations

More mushrooms: If you're a mushroom lover, omit the tofu, lima beans, and asparagus and double the mushrooms.

Serve with a simple green salad and warm baguette as a complete meal.

Hands-on prep time: 20 minutes
Cook time: 25 minutes (including pasta cook time)
Total time: 35 minutes
Makes about 10 cups

Ingredients

- ¼ **pound fettuccine,** broken into 2-inch pieces
- 2 **Tbsp butter or oil**
- ¼ **cup chopped onion**
- 2 **cups sliced porcini, cremini, and/or portobello mushrooms**
- 1 **Tbsp minced garlic** (2-3 cloves)
- 1 **Tbsp unbleached white flour**
- 4 **cups water**
- 1¾ **tsp salt or to taste**
- 2½-**ounce chunk fresh parmesan cheese** plus extra grated for garnishing
- 1 **cup bite-size broccoli florets**
- 1 **cup chopped asparagus,** bases trimmed
- ½ **cup frozen lima beans** (optional)
- 3 **Tbsp sherry** (optional)
- **Fresh-ground black pepper to taste**
- 6 **sprigs fresh tarragon** (or 2 tsp dried)
- 1 **cup half-and-half** (cream)
- 1 **cup finely cubed extra-firm tofu** (optional)
- 2 **cups chopped spinach** (tightly packed)

Wild Rice & Yam Potage

Here's a beautiful, cozy soup to make winter guests feel right at home. Rich in protein and B vitamins, wild rice imparts an earthy, nutty flavor that goes naturally with grounding root vegetables like yam and rutabaga.

Plan ahead: This recipe calls for Italian Broth (p. 281).

Procedure

1. Place the broth and wild rice in a 5-quart pot over high heat. Bring to a boil, reduce the heat to medium, cover, and simmer for about 50 minutes.

2. Add the yam, rutabaga, apricot, peppercorns, vinegar, and 2 teaspoons of the Spike. Simmer for another 25 minutes or until the rice and yams are tender.

3. Meanwhile, heat the oil in a medium skillet over high heat. Add the mushrooms and remaining 1 teaspoon Spike and sauté for a few minutes until the mushrooms begin to brown. Add the rapini and fennel seeds and sauté for a few more minutes until the rapini wilts. Add the sautéed mushrooms and rapini to the soup, reserving some of the rapini for garnishing (optional). Ladle the soup into bowls, garnish, and serve.

Tips/Variations

Broth variation: To make this recipe without the Italian Broth, use an equal amount of water instead and add 2 veggie bouillon cubes, 2 tablespoons parmesan cheese, 1 to 2 tablespoons tomato paste, and a handful of fresh basil leaves.

Rapini variation: You can substitute arugula or spinach for the rapini.

Make it a meal: Top or serve with Seasoned TVP Nuggets (p. 293). A warm loaf of bread is also a natural accompaniment.

Hands-on prep time: 25 minutes
Cook time: 1 hour 25 minutes (not including Italian Broth time)
Total time: 1 hour 30 minutes
Makes about 10 cups

Ingredients

10 cups Italian Broth (p. 281)

1 cup uncooked wild rice

2½ cups cubed yam (1-2 yams)

1½ cups peeled, cubed rutabaga (1-2 rutabagas)

3 Tbsp finely sliced dried apricot

¼ tsp black peppercorns

2 tsp balsamic vinegar

3 tsp Spike or to taste

1 Tbsp oil

1 cup sliced cremini, portobello, or button mushrooms

3 cups roughly torn rapini (1 bunch, tough bottom stems removed)

½ tsp fennel seeds

Ribollita

According to my friends, this recipe is one of the best in the book. The secret to its deliciousness lies in a gorgeous garlicky Italian broth. Literally meaning "reboiled," ribollita is also known as tuscan bread soup. It is said by some to taste best when reboiled for the third time, so you can look forward to any leftovers!

Plan ahead: This recipe requires Italian Broth (p. 281).

Procedure

1. Heat the oil in a 5-quart pot over high heat. Add the leek and sauté for a few minutes until it begins to brown. Add the basil and sauté for a few more seconds.

2. Add the remaining ingredients except the croutons and bring to a boil. Reduce the heat to medium, cover, and simmer for 5 minutes. Meanwhile, prepare the croutons.

3. Remove from the heat, ladle into bowls, and serve with croutons in the soup or on the side.

Tips/Variations

Leftovers: Add leftover croutons to leftover soup. When you reheat it the next day, bring the soup to a boil, then reduce the heat to medium-low, cover, and simmer for 15 to 20 minutes, stirring occasionally. At this point, the bread and soup have become one and the soup has an entirely different consistency.

> **Hands-on prep time:** 15 minutes
> **Cook time:** 30 minutes (not including Italian Broth time)
> **Total time:** 35 minutes
> **Makes** about 12 cups

Ingredients

2 Tbsp oil
½ cup finely sliced leek
2 dozen whole basil leaves
2 cups chopped roma tomato
  (4-6 tomatoes)
1½ tsp salt or to taste
¾ tsp whole black peppercorns
3 Tbsp chopped Italian parsley
3 large cloves garlic, sliced
10 cups Italian Broth (p. 281)
1 recipe Italian Croutons (p. 288)

Asian

Whether you're a fan of Thai, Chinese, Japanese, or Vietnamese cuisine, you'll find the flavors of your favorite Asian restaurants made easy and attainable right in your own kitchen.

Lotus Root Udon Noodle Soup

Lacy lotus root can make any dish beautiful. Combined with colorful veggies and hearty udon noodles in a light, tasty Asian broth, the result is a satisfying, low-fat soup with fresh, clean flavors. This lovely soup also benefits your lungs and immune system.

Procedure

1. Heat the oil in a 4-quart pot over high heat. Add the onion, garlic, and ginger and sauté for a few minutes until they begin to brown.

2. Add the water, beans or broccoli, carrot, bell pepper, and lotus root and bring to a boil. Reduce the heat to medium, cover, and simmer for about 10 minutes.

3. Add the udon noodles, increase the heat to high, and return to a boil. Reduce the heat to medium, stir with a fork to separate the noodles, and simmer for another 10 minutes or so.

4. Add the seaweed (optional), coriander, salt, soy sauce, and vinegar and stir through. Remove from the heat and let sit for 5 minutes before serving. Add a bit more water if necessary and adjust the salt accordingly. Add the snow peas, ladle into bowls, and serve.

Tips/Variations

Make it a meal: Top or serve with Teriyaki Tofu or Seitan l'Orange (both on p. 292). Daikon Slaw (p. 297) is also great on the side.

Serve with hoisin and sriracha sauces, as well as a set of chopsticks.

> Hands-on prep time: 15 minutes
> Cook time: 30 minutes
> Total time: 45 minutes (including "sit" time)
> Makes about 7 cups

Ingredients

1 Tbsp toasted sesame oil

½ cup thinly sliced onion

1½ Tbsp minced garlic
(3-4 cloves)

1 Tbsp minced ginger

6 cups water

1 cup chopped green beans
or broccoli, fresh or frozen

½ cup julienned carrot

½ cup slivered red bell pepper

20 rounds lotus root
(¼-inch thick)

3 ounces dry udon noodles

2 tsp shredded dried wakame
seaweed (optional)

1½ tsp ground coriander

1 tsp salt or to taste

¼ cup soy sauce

1½ Tbsp rice vinegar

10 snow peas, julienned
(strings removed)

Teriyaki Soup

This simple, mellow soup makes a nourishing meal for any season. Rich in B vitamins, it goes over well with both kids and adults. The tofu is out of this world, so go ahead and triple it if you'd like extra.

Procedure

1. Heat the oil in a 6-quart pot over high heat. Add the onion, garlic, and mushrooms and sauté for a few minutes until the mushrooms just begin to brown.

2. Add the water, rice, ginger, pepper, salt, and soy sauce. Bring to a boil, reduce the heat to medium-low, cover, and simmer for 45 minutes or until the rice is just tender. Meanwhile, prepare the Teriyaki Tofu (p. 292).

3. When the rice is just tender, add the remaining ingredients except the tofu, increase the heat to high, and bring to a boil. Remove from the heat. Add a little extra water if necessary and adjust the salt accordingly. Ladle into bowls, top each with 6 to 8 pieces of tofu and sprinklings of green onion, mint or cilantro, and sesame seeds, and serve.

Tips/Variations

If you know you'll have leftovers: This recipe yields a big pot, so if you're not feeding a crowd, you may wish to cook the rice separately and add it to individual portions so it doesn't absorb all the broth once leftovers are stored. If you do this, reduce the water by 2 cups.

Serve with condiments like hoisin and sriracha sauces, gomasio, and/or wedges of fresh lime. The spicy Slimming Slaw (p. 296) also goes nicely on the side.

Hands-on prep time: 25 minutes
Cook time: 1 hour
Total time: 1 hour 5 minutes
Makes about 14 cups

Ingredients

3 Tbsp toasted sesame oil

1 cup slivered onion

2 Tbsp minced garlic (4-6 cloves)

1 cup sliced shiitake mushrooms (stems removed)

10 cups water

1 cup short grain brown rice

¼ cup minced ginger

½ tsp white pepper

2 tsp salt or to taste

¼ cup soy sauce

2 Tbsp sugar

1 cup chopped celery (2 stalks)

1 cup julienned or chopped carrot (1-2 carrots)

2 cups chopped baby bok choy (2 small bunches)

1 cup julienned snow peas (strings removed)

2 cups bean sprouts (chopped or whole)

2 recipes Teriyaki Tofu (p. 292)

Garnishes

⅓ cup minced green onion (4-5 onions)

⅓ cup minced mint leaves or cilantro

2 Tbsp toasted sesame seeds*

*See Toasting Nuts and Seeds, p. 10.

Thai Carrot Soup

This soup is sweet, savory, spicy, and aromatic all rolled into one. It has a silken, full-bodied coconut-creamy texture that makes it an absolute pleasure for the palate. It's a soup I'm often asked to make, so I'm grateful it's so simple.

Procedure

1. Place the water, salt, carrot, celery, lemongrass, lime leaves (optional), ginger, garlic, and soy sauce in a 5-quart pot and bring to a boil over high heat. Reduce the heat to medium-low, cover, and simmer for 10 minutes or until the carrots are tender.

2. Stir in the coconut milk and cilantro (optional) and remove from the heat. In batches, place in a blender and blend until smooth. Return to the pot and add the corn. Bring to a quick boil and remove from the heat. Ladle into bowls, garnish with the green onion and coconut (optional), and serve.

Tips/Variations

Carrot tip: If your carrots aren't very flavorful, add a veggie bouillon cube and some sugar to taste.

Make it even richer by blending with a cup of roasted unsalted cashews.

Hands-on prep time: 15 minutes
Cook time: 20 minutes
Total time: 35 minutes
Makes about 10 cups

Ingredients

6 cups water

1½ tsp salt or to taste

7 cups roughly chopped carrot (8-10 carrots)

1½ cups roughly chopped celery (3 stalks)

1 stalk lemongrass, chopped* (base, tough outer layers, and dry tops removed)

4 small kaffir lime leaves, deveined* (optional)

¼ cup roughly chopped ginger (3-inch piece)

1 large clove garlic

¼ cup soy sauce or to taste

One 14-ounce can coconut milk

1 cup cilantro (loosely packed, optional)

2 cups frozen corn

3 Tbsp minced green onion for garnishing

¼ cup toasted desiccated coconut** for garnishing (optional)

*See Preparing Lemongrass and Kaffir Lime Leaf, both on p. 12.

**To toast the coconut, place in a small dry skillet over medium heat. Toast for 1 to 2 minutes, stirring often, until the flecks become golden and fragrant. Remove from the heat and transfer to a dish.

Vegetable Pho

This impressive mountain of fresh herbs, veggies, noodles, and scrumptious caramelized tofu is a beautiful sight to behold—especially when presented as your dinner. Inspired by a traditional Vietnamese soup, this spectacular meal-in-itself is fun to assemble and quite easy to make.

Procedure

1. Heat the oil in a 6-quart pot over high heat. Add the onion and sauté for a few minutes until it begins to brown. Add the garlic and sauté for another minute.

2. Add the remaining ingredients except the broccoli, snow peas, noodles, and tofu or seitan and bring to a boil. Reduce the heat to medium, cover, and simmer for 10 minutes.

3. Raise the heat to high, bring to a boil, and add the broccoli, snow peas, and noodles. Reduce the heat to medium and let the soup simmer for as long as directed on the noodle package (do not overcook!). Meanwhile, prepare the tofu or seitan.

4. Ladle into large bowls (you can use tongs as well), garnish with sprouts, fresh herbs, tofu or seitan, and peanuts (in that order), and serve.

Tips/Variations

Star variation: If you have star anise on hand, add 2 or 3 whole stars in Step 2.

Getting the perfect bite: Each person should have a ramekin that has equal amounts of hoisin and sriracha chili sauces side by side. Lightly dip your chopsticks or spoon into both sauces just before dipping into the soup to take a bite.

> **Hands-on prep time:** 40 minutes
> **Cook time:** 30 minutes
> **Total time:** 45 minutes
> **Makes** about 14 cups soup plus add-ins
>   (8 meal-size bowls)

Ingredients

3 Tbsp bland oil
2 cups slivered onion (2 onions)
3 Tbsp sliced garlic (6-9 cloves)
8 cups water
2-3 vegetarian beef or chicken bouillon cubes
1 cinnamon stick
2 Tbsp minced ginger
½ cup tamari or soy sauce
1 Tbsp sugar
2 Tbsp rice vinegar
1 cup chopped celery (2 stalks)
1 cup chopped carrot (1-2 carrots)
4 cups shredded napa cabbage or bok choy
Salt to taste
3½ cups chopped broccoli
2 dozen snow peas (strings removed)
7 ounces dried linguine-size rice noodles
2 recipes Teriyaki Tofu or Seitan l'Orange (both on p. 292)

Garnishes

4 cups chopped bean sprouts
4 cups fresh herbs (like Thai basil, cilantro, and/or mint)
¾ cup chopped roasted peanuts
Hoisin and sriracha sauces for serving

Malaysian Peanut Soup

Quick and straightforward to make, this delectable symphony of spices and flavors gives you a rich, tangy broth in minutes—thanks to peanut butter, coconut, tomato, and tamarind. Look for tamarind paste in Asian markets, health food stores, and well-stocked grocery stores. Served with a bowl of rice, this soup is easily a meal.

Procedure

1. Heat the oil in a 6-quart pot over high heat. Add the onion and sauté for a few minutes until it begins to brown. Add the garlic and peppercorns and sauté for another minute.

2. Add the remaining ingredients except the coconut cream and bring to a boil. Reduce the heat to medium, cover, and simmer for 15 to 20 minutes. Stir in the coconut cream and remove from the heat. Remove the lemongrass, ladle into bowls, and serve.

Tips/Variations

Cashew variation: If someone at your table has a peanut allergy, use cashew butter instead of peanut butter.

Garnish possibilities: Chopped bean sprouts, diced cucumber, fresh herbs (like cilantro, mint, or Thai basil), and/or peanuts (or cashews).

Make it a meal: Serve with Seitan L'Orange (p. 292) and basmati rice. If you're in a rush and want to make the soup more substantial, you can add 2 cups cubed firm or deep-fried tofu in Step 2. (Deep-fried tofu can be found in Asian markets and some grocery stores.)

> Hands-on prep time: 20 minutes
> Cook time: 35 minutes
> Total time: 50 minutes
> Makes about 12 cups

Ingredients

1 Tbsp bland oil

1 cup slivered onion

2 Tbsp minced garlic (4-6 cloves)

½ tsp whole black peppercorns

8 cups water

1 stalk lemongrass, crushed*
(use a rolling pin)

2 tsp ground coriander

½ tsp ground cumin

¼ tsp turmeric

½ tsp cinnamon

½ tsp minced fresh chili
or red chili flakes

2 tsp sugar

2½ tsp salt or to taste

1 Tbsp tamarind paste

3 Tbsp tomato paste

1 cup diced tomato

5 cups chopped broccoli,
including peeled stems
(1 bunch)

4 cups chopped swiss chard
or spinach (packed)

1 cup diced red bell pepper

⅓ cup unsalted peanut butter

1 Tbsp minced ginger

One 14-ounce can coconut
cream

*See Preparing Lemongrass, p. 12.

Jade Curry

Spicy and flavorful, this versatile soup can be made with different vegetables, depending on what's available. I originally made it with green papaya, which grows right in our backyard in Hawaii. When I venture into colder climates, however, green papaya is not always a common find, so I'll use potato or even jerusalem artichoke instead. Enzyme-rich green papaya is simply unripe regular papaya. It has a mild and pleasant peppery flavor. If you find it in Chinatown, give it a try.

Procedure

1. Heat the oil in a 5-quart pot over medium-high heat. Add the onion, garlic, ginger, lemongrass, and curry paste and sauté for a few minutes until they begin to brown. Add the potato or papaya and sauté for another couple of minutes.

2. Add 5 cups of the water and the tofu, sugar, and salt, increase the heat to high, and bring to a boil. Reduce the heat to medium, cover, and simmer for 15 minutes. Add the bell pepper, beans or broccoli, and coconut milk and simmer for another 10 minutes.

3. Combine the remaining ¼ cup water with the cornstarch until a smooth paste is formed. Add this to the soup, stirring constantly to make sure no lumps form. Remove from the heat and remove the lemongrass. Ladle into bowls and serve.

> **Hands-on prep time:** 15 minutes
> **Cook time:** 35 minutes
> **Total time:** 45 minutes
> **Makes** about 10 cups

Ingredients

2 Tbsp bland oil

1 cup chopped onion

1 large clove garlic, sliced

2 Tbsp minced ginger

4-5 whole stalks lemongrass, crushed (use a rolling pin)

1½ Tbsp vegetarian green curry paste

5 cups cubed potato or green papaya (peeled and seeded)

5¼ cups water

1½ cups cubed firm tofu

2 tsp sugar

3 tsp salt

1 cup chopped red bell pepper

1 cup chopped green beans or broccoli, fresh or frozen

One 14-ounce can coconut milk

2 Tbsp cornstarch

Blushing Thai Curry

Once you discover tom yum paste (also known as hot and sour paste), you'll find yourself achieving the flavors of your favorite Thai restaurant right in your own kitchen. A mixture of chili, galangal (Thai ginger), lemongrass, and kaffir lime leaf, tom yum infuses this spicy, luscious coconut-based soup with its distinct flavor and aroma. I love Asian curry pastes like tom yum because they create an incredible depth of flavor in a very short time.

Procedure

1. Heat the oil in a 6-quart pot over medium-high heat. Add the onion and garlic and sauté for a few minutes until they begin to brown. Add the tom yum paste and sauté for another 30 seconds.

2. Add the water, tomato, potato, salt, and sugar. Increase the heat to high and bring to a boil. Reduce the heat to medium-low, cover, and simmer for about 20 minutes.

3. Add the bell pepper and coconut milk and simmer for another 10 minutes. Remove from the heat, add the cilantro or basil and tofu, and stir through. Ladle into bowls and serve.

Tips/Variations

Serve with steamed rice and a mild julienned cucumber salad.

> **Hands-on prep time:** 15 minutes
> **Cook time:** 45 minutes
> **Total time:** 55 minutes
> **Makes** about 12 cups

Ingredients

1 Tbsp bland oil

2 cups diced onion (2 onions)

2 Tbsp minced garlic (4-6 cloves)

3 Tbsp vegetarian tom yum paste*

7 cups water

One 28-ounce can diced tomato (or 3½ cups fresh)

3 cups cubed red potato (3 potatoes)

1 Tbsp salt or to taste

1 Tbsp sugar

1 cup chopped red bell pepper

One 14-ounce can coconut milk

1 cup chopped cilantro or Thai basil

2 cups cubed extra-firm or deep-fried tofu**

*Tom yum paste is available in most Asian markets and some health food stores. You can also use vegetarian red curry paste instead.

**You can buy packaged deep-fried tofu in all Asian markets and some grocery stores.

Easy Indian Curry

It's hard to go wrong with this simple and sumptuous curry. Just be discriminating in choosing your curry powder. Some curry powders from the Far East use too much fenugreek, making a dish bitter and even unpleasant. The perfect curry has balanced flavors and isn't dominated by any one, least of all the bitter flavor. Many curry powders from India and Pakistan are safe bets, especially a nice madras.

Procedure

1. Heat the ghee, butter, or oil in a 5-quart pot over high heat. Add the onion and garlic and sauté for a couple of minutes until they begin to brown.

2. Add the water, squash, chickpeas, sugar, salt, and 2 teaspoons of the curry powder. Bring to a boil, reduce the heat to medium, cover, and simmer for 10 minutes. Add the cashews, raisins (optional), and florets and simmer for 10 minutes or until the florets are tender.

3. Add the peas and half-and-half or coconut milk, increase the heat to high, and bring to a quick boil. Reduce the heat to medium and simmer for a few minutes. Remove from the heat, add the remaining 1 teaspoon curry powder and cilantro or mint, and stir through. Ladle into bowls and serve.

Tips/Variations

Serve with basmati rice, baked samosas, and Mango Chutney (p. 295).

Hands-on prep time: 15 minutes
Cook time: 30 minutes
Total time: 40 minutes
Makes about 8 cups

Ingredients

1-2 Tbsp ghee, butter, or oil

½ cup slivered onion

1 Tbsp minced garlic (2-3 cloves)

4¼ cups water

2 cups cubed butternut or kabocha squash

2¼ cups cooked or canned chickpeas (rinsed and drained)

2 tsp sugar

2 tsp salt or to taste

3 tsp madras curry powder

½ cup roasted unsalted cashews

3 Tbsp sultana raisins (optional)

2 cups bite-size romanesco,* cauliflower, or broccoflower florets

½ cup frozen peas

1 cup half-and-half (cream) or coconut milk

¼ cup minced cilantro or mint leaves

*Romanesco looks somewhat like green cauliflower except that its florets are pointy.

Watercress Rice Noodle Soup

Filled with tofu, shiitake mushrooms, watercress, and noodles, this healthy and attractive soup makes a satisfying meal. The broth is simple and tasty, though you can add a couple of kaffir lime leaves or a splash of rice vinegar if you're in the mood for a bit more zing.

Procedure

1. Heat the oil in a 4-quart pot over high heat. Add the onion and sauté for a few minutes until it begins to brown. Add the garlic, mushroom, and bell pepper and sauté for another minute or so.

2. Add the water, salt, and tofu. Bring to a boil, reduce the heat to medium, cover, and simmer for about 15 minutes.

3. Add the rice noodles, tomato, chili, and soy sauce and simmer for another minute, then remove from the heat. Allow to sit for a couple of minutes to let the noodles soften. Stir in the watercress, ladle into bowls, and serve.

Tips/Variations

If you're not serving immediately: Cook the noodles separately and add them just before serving so they won't soak up all the broth. Reduce the water by ¾ cup. Add the watercress to individual bowls so it stays zesty and crisp and doesn't overpower the broth.

Tofu variation: Replace the plain tofu with Teriyaki Tofu or Seitan l'Orange (both on p. 292) and add it at the end, just before serving.

Hands-on prep time: 10 minutes
Cook time: 35 minutes
Total time: 40 minutes
Makes about 8 cups

Ingredients

1 Tbsp toasted sesame oil

1 cup slivered onion

1 Tbsp minced garlic (2-3 cloves)

1 cup finely sliced shiitake mushrooms (stems removed)

¾ cup slivered red bell pepper

6 cups water

1 tsp salt or to taste

1 cup cubed soft or firm tofu

2 ounces dried rice vermicelli

1 cup chopped tomato (1-2 tomatoes)

½ tsp minced fresh chili or red chili flakes (optional)

¼ cup soy sauce

1 cup finely chopped watercress (or more if desired)

Laotian Curry

When you're short on energy, this easy one-pot wonder yields a big pot with minimum effort. Fans of Southeast Asian cooking will love the rich coconutty broth and tender cauliflower and eggplant.

Procedure

1. Heat the oil in a 6-quart pot over high heat. Add the onion and sauté for a few minutes until it begins to brown. Add the garlic and mustard seeds and sauté for another minute.

2. Add the remaining ingredients except the coconut milk, spinach, and cilantro or basil and bring to boil. Reduce the heat to medium-low, cover, and simmer for about 20 minutes.

3. Add the coconut milk, spinach, and cilantro or basil and simmer for another 5 minutes or so. Remove from the heat, ladle into bowls, and serve.

Tips/Variations

Spice it up: Add a minced fresh chili at the very end if you like it spicy.

Make it a meal: In Step 2, add 2 cups of cubed firm or deep-fried tofu (which you'll find in Asian markets and some grocery stores). Serve with scoops of jasmine or Thai sticky rice on the side—or even in the soup.

> Hands-on prep time: 15 minutes
> Cook time: 35 minutes
> Total time: 45 minutes
> Makes about 11 cups

Ingredients

- 1 Tbsp bland oil
- 2 cups diced onion (2 onions)
- 1 Tbsp minced garlic (2-3 cloves)
- ½ tsp black mustard seeds
- 2 cups bite-size cauliflower florets
- 2 cups cubed Asian eggplant
- 1 cup chopped carrot (1-2 carrots)
- One 28-ounce can diced tomato (or 3½ cups fresh)
- 4 cups water
- ½ tsp ground cumin
- 1 tsp ground coriander
- 1 tsp curry powder
- 2 tsp salt or to taste
- 1 Tbsp sugar
- ½ stick cinnamon
- 2 Tbsp rice vinegar
- One 14-ounce can coconut milk
- 2 cups whole baby spinach leaves
- ½ cup chopped cilantro or Thai basil (packed)

Wonton Min

Don't let this soup intimidate you. All my friends who tested this recipe were surprised at how easy it really is. A common find in North American noodle houses, Wonton Min refers to a meal-sized soup packed with vegetables, wonton dumplings, and noodles. Vary the veggies according to what you've got in the crisper and enjoy healthy, homemade Chinese.

Procedure

1. Prepare the wontons (see next page).

2. When the wontons are done, heat the oil in a 6-quart pot over high heat. Add the onion and sauté for a few minutes until it begins to brown. Add the celery, mushrooms, and garlic and sauté for another few minutes until the mushrooms begin to brown.

3. Add the pepper, salt, soy sauce, and water and bring to a boil. Add the beans or snow peas, greens, and noodles and cook for 4 minutes or until the noodles are just done. Add the cilantro or mint and remove from the heat.

4. Ladle into large bowls, top with wontons (4 to 5 per bowl), garnish with green onion and a drizzle of toasted sesame oil, and serve.

Tips/Variations

Veggie variation: Skip the noodles and add an extra 2 cups of your favorite vegetables.

Noodle variation: If you prefer, use 3 ounces of dried rice noodles instead of ramen. You may need to cook them a few minutes longer.

Serve with chopsticks and condiments like hoisin sauce or sweet chili sauce.

Hands-on prep time: 50-60 minutes
Cook time: 30 minutes
Total time: 1 hour 30 minutes
Makes about 12 cups plus 24 wontons

Ingredients

1 recipe Wontons (p. 144)

2 Tbsp toasted sesame oil
plus extra for garnishing

½ cup slivered onion

1 cup chopped celery (2 stalks)

1 cup sliced button or shiitake mushrooms

1½ Tbsp minced garlic (3-4 cloves)

Dash of white pepper

2 tsp salt or to taste

3 Tbsp soy sauce

10 cups water

¾ cup chopped Chinese long beans or snow peas

2 cups chopped greens (like spinach, napa cabbage, or bok choy, packed)

One 3-ounce package dried ramen noodles, broken up

½ cup chopped cilantro or mint leaves (tightly packed)

2 Tbsp minced green onion for garnishing

Ingredients

1 Tbsp toasted sesame oil

½ cup chopped onion

1 tsp minced garlic

1 cup chopped mushrooms

½ tsp salt

¼ tsp dried thyme

¼ tsp black pepper

⅔ cup ground roasted
unsalted almonds

2 tsp minced ginger

4 Tbsp water

3 Tbsp minced water chestnut

3 Tbsp minced green onion

3 Tbsp minced cilantro or
mint leaves

1 Tbsp cornstarch

1 package eggless wonton
wrappers*

*You can buy eggless wonton
wrappers in any Asian market
and some grocery stores.

Wontons

Procedure

1. Heat the oil in a medium skillet over high heat. Add the onion and sauté for a few minutes until it begins to brown. Add the garlic, mushrooms, salt, thyme, and pepper and sauté for a few minutes more. Remove from the heat, then place in a blender or food processor along with the ground almonds, ginger, and 3 tablespoons of the water and blend until quite smooth (do not overblend or it will become too pasty).

2. Place the mixture in a 2-quart bowl and add the water chestnut, green onion, and cilantro or mint and mix well.

3. Combine the cornstarch and remaining 1 tablespoon water to form a smooth paste. Wet the edges of each wonton wrapper with the paste. Place a rounded teaspoon of filling in the center of each wrapper, fold the wrapper over to create a half moon, and press the edges together to seal it. Bring the far 2 corners together and tie or roll them together, pressing so the corners stick together.

4. In a wide pot or deep skillet, bring 2 inches of water to a boil over high heat. Place the wontons in the boiling water in batches, being careful not to overlap them (as they may stick together). Boil for 1 minute, remove from the water, and set aside on a plate, again being careful not to overlap them.

Fun

Young, old, or somewhere in between, everyone
will love these easy and delicious crowd-pleasers.

Alphabet Soup

This simple, familiar classic always evokes a smile. With mellow, wholesome flavors that appeal to kids of all ages, Alphabet Soup is a great everyday dish that's well received any time of year.

Procedure

1. Heat the oil in a 4-quart pot over medium-high heat. Add the celery and bell pepper and sauté for a few minutes until browning. Add the tomato and cook for a few more minutes. Transfer to a blender, blend until smooth, and return to the pot.

2. Add the remaining ingredients except the parsley and cheese and bring to a boil. Reduce the heat to medium, cover, and simmer for about 10 minutes or until the pasta is cooked.

3. Add the parsley (optional) and stir through. Ladle into bowls, garnish with parmesan or cream cheese (optional), and serve.

Tips/Variations

For adults: Try serving with a crostini (p. 286) or Savory Croutons (p. 288; kids like these too). You can also add minced fresh chili to taste.

> Hands-on prep time: 15 minutes
> Cook time: 25 minutes
> Total time: 40 minutes
> Makes about 9 cups

Ingredients

1 Tbsp oil

¾ cup chopped celery (1-2 stalks)

1¼ cups chopped red bell pepper

One 28-ounce can diced tomato (or 3½ cups fresh)

6 cups water

1 veggie bouillon cube

1 tsp garlic powder

1 tsp onion powder

1½ tsp salt or to taste

1½ tsp Italian seasoning

½ cup alphabet pasta

1½ cups fresh or frozen mixed vegetables

¼ cup tomato paste

1 Tbsp sugar

¼ cup minced Italian parsley (optional)

Parmesan cheese or small cubes of cream cheese for garnishing (optional)

Daydream Soup

This easy vegetarian "chicken with rice" is tailor-made for young tastebuds. With nurturing basmati rice and delicious little pastry puffs, it's a satisfying lunch or supper your whole family will welcome.

Procedure

1. Preheat the oven to 350°F. Roll the pastry sheet ⅛ inch thick and use cookie cutters to cut out fun shapes. Spread on an ungreased cookie sheet and refrigerate for 15 minutes.

2. Heat 1 tablespoon of the butter or oil in a 5-quart pot over medium-high heat. Add the rice and toast for a minute. Add the water, potato, bouillon cubes, Spike, yeast, and 2 tablespoons of the Braggs; then raise the heat to high and bring to a boil. Reduce the heat to medium-low, cover, and cook for 10 to 15 minutes or until the rice and potato are tender.

3. Place the pastry puffs in the oven and bake for 12 minutes or until golden with a hint of brown.

4. Meanwhile, heat the remaining 1 tablespoon butter or oil in a medium skillet over medium-high heat. Add the tofu and the remaining 1 tablespoon Braggs and pan-fry for 5 to 7 minutes, stirring occasionally, until the tofu is golden on most sides. Remove from the heat.

5. Add the veggies to the soup and simmer for 5 more minutes. Add a little extra water and salt if necessary. Stir in the tofu and remove from the heat. Ladle into bowls, top with pastry puffs, and serve.

Tips/Variations

Veggie chicken variation: Cube 2 or 3 vegetarian chicken burgers and pan-fry them in place of the tofu.

> Hands-on prep time: 20 minutes
> Cook time: 35 minutes
> Total time: 45 minutes
> Makes about 10 cups

Ingredients

- 1 package Pepperidge Farm (or other) puff pastry sheets, thawed
- 2 Tbsp butter or oil
- 1 cup basmati rice (or other white rice)
- 8 cups water
- 1 cup cubed potato
- 2 veggie chicken bouillon cubes
- 1 Tbsp Spike
- 2 Tbsp nutritional yeast
- 3 Tbsp Bragg Liquid Aminos or to taste
- 1 cup finely cubed extra-firm tofu
- ½ cup frozen carrots and peas

Mac 'n Cheese Soup

When my kids were younger and their friends stayed for mealtimes, this was one foolproof recipe that could get even the fussiest eater asking for seconds. If anyone is dairy-sensitive, try adding cooked macaroni to Creamy Cashew Soup (p. 73) instead; it's equally delicious.

Procedure

1. Place the water, Spike, pepper, and mustard in a 4-quart pot and bring to a boil over high heat. Add the macaroni and cook for 10 minutes or until the pasta is just done.

2. Combine the milk or half-and-half with the flour until smooth. Add this to the soup, stirring constantly to make sure no lumps form. Add the veggies and bring to a boil. Reduce the heat to medium and simmer for a couple of minutes, then remove from the heat.

3. Add the cheese, stir until melted, and salt to taste if necessary. Ladle into bowls, garnish with bread crumbs or croutons and parmesan cheese, and serve.

Tips/Variations

Cheese variation: Cheese lovers may want to try this recipe with more exotic alternatives like fontina, aged gruyère, or gouda.

Additional garnishes: Garnish with simulated bacon bits and a dash of paprika.

Serve with buttered wholegrain toast and dill pickles.

Hands-on prep time: 5 minutes
Cook time: 15 minutes
Total time: 20 minutes
Makes about 8½ cups

Ingredients

6 cups water

1 Tbsp Spike

½ tsp black pepper

2 tsp dry mustard

2 cups dried macaroni noodles

2 cups milk or half-and-half (cream)

¼ cup unbleached white flour

2 cups frozen veggies (like carrots, peas, and green beans)

2 cups grated cheddar cheese (8 ounces)

Salt to taste

1 cup wholegrain bread crumbs or Savory Croutons (p. 288) for garnishing

¼ cup parmesan cheese for garnishing

I Love Peanut Butter Soup

I love using peanut butter to thicken savory soups. It creates a full body and a gentle flavor that works well with most vegetables. Try it in this easy everyday recipe.

Procedure

1. Place the water, salt, celery, carrot, potato, peanut butter, and pepper in a 4-quart pot and bring to a boil over high heat. Reduce the heat to medium, cover, and simmer for about 15 minutes until the potato is tender.

2. Ladle 2 cups soup into a blender, blend until smooth, and return to the pot. Add the corn and zucchini and simmer for another 5 to 10 minutes. Remove from the heat, ladle into bowls, garnish with peanuts (optional), and serve.

Tips/Variations

Nut variation: This soup is also delicious with cashew or almond butter instead of peanut butter and toasted cashews or almonds as a garnish instead of peanuts.

Asian variation: Add 2 teaspoons of green curry paste and garnish with diced cucumber.

Make it a meal: Top or serve with Teriyaki Tofu (p. 292) or Seasoned TVP Nuggets (p. 293). Buttered wholegrain toast is great on the side.

> **Hands-on prep time:** 10 minutes
> **Cook time:** 30 minutes
> **Total time:** 35 minutes
> **Makes** about 8 cups

Ingredients

- 5 cups water
- 2 tsp salt or to taste
- 1 cup diced celery (2 stalks)
- 1 cup diced carrot (1-2 carrots)
- 4 cups chopped potato (3-4 potatoes)
- ½ cup unsalted peanut butter
- ¼ tsp black pepper or to taste
- 1 cup frozen corn
- ½ cup diced zucchini
- 2 Tbsp chopped roasted salted peanuts (optional)

Volcano Soup

My kids created this fun soup when they were young. You can probably see where they got the name for it. With uncomplicated, satisfying flavors, it's a comforting recipe that tastes like good ol' home cooking. The gravy is out of this world, especially if you use chickpea flour (besan).

Procedure

1. Place the potato, water, and 1 teaspoon of the salt in a 5-quart pot and bring to a boil over high heat. Reduce the heat to medium, cover, and simmer for 10 to 15 minutes until the potato is tender. Meanwhile, prepare the gravy (see next page).

2. Remove 6 cups of the boiled potato and place in a 3-quart mixing bowl with ½ cup of the sour cream, the butter, and the remaining ¾ teaspoon salt. Mash together until smooth and fluffy.

3. In batches, place the remaining potato, the potato water, the remaining ½ cup of sour cream, and the turmeric in a blender and blend until smooth. Do not overblend or it will become gluey. Return to the pot, cover, simmer over medium heat for 5 minutes, and remove from the heat.

4. To serve, create a mountain of mashed potatoes in the center of each bowl. Ladle soup around the mountain. Use a chopstick to make a finger-sized hole down the center of the mountain. Use a baster or measuring cup with a good spout to fill the hole with gravy, letting the mountain erupt like a volcano. Yum!

Tips/Variations

Make it a meal: Top or serve with Seasoned TVP Nuggets (p. 293). A creamy coleslaw makes a scrumptious side dish.

> **Hands-on prep time:** 30 minutes
> **Cook time:** 40 minutes
> **Total time:** 1 hour
> **Makes** about 7 cups soup, 6 cups mashed potatoes, and 4 cups gravy (4-6 servings)

Ingredients

11 cups peeled, chopped potato (8-10 potatoes)
6 cups water
1¾ tsp salt or to taste
1 cup sour cream
2 Tbsp butter
½ tsp turmeric
1 recipe Geyser Gravy (p. 158)

Beautiful Besan
Besan or chickpea flour has a rich nutty flavor that makes a perfect gravy base. Also known as gram, chana flour, and garbanzo flour, it is a key ingredient in papadams (a crispy East Indian flatbread) as well as many East Indian desserts. It's also used in some Mediterranean cooking. You'll find it in health food stores, gourmet grocery stores, and East Indian markets.

Geyser Gravy

Ingredients

½ cup butter
¾ cup chickpea flour or unbleached white flour
4 cups water
2 Tbsp soy sauce
¾ tsp poultry seasoning
¼ tsp black pepper
2 Tbsp nutritional yeast (optional but very tasty)
¼ tsp salt or to taste
½ tsp garlic powder
½ tsp onion powder

Procedure

1. Melt the butter in a 2-quart saucepan over medium heat. Add the flour and toast for 3 to 5 minutes or so, stirring often, until it becomes fragrant and almond-colored.

2. Add the water 1 cup at a time, whisking constantly to prevent lumps from forming. If it's thickening too fast, you can briefly take it off the heat and whisk rapidly to make it smooth and creamy; then put it back on the heat and finish adding the water.

3. Add the remaining ingredients, stir well, and bring to a boil. Reduce the heat to low, cover, and simmer for a few minutes. Remove from the heat. Give it a good stir before serving and add a little more water if necessary.

Nacho Bean Soup

If you have growing kids in the house, this generous recipe will have them coming back for seconds and thirds. Hearty and cheesy, it's a thick, delicious black bean soup that tastes even better the next day.

Procedure

1. Heat the oil in an 8-quart pot over high heat. Add the onion, garlic, celery, and bell pepper and sauté for a few minutes until they begin to brown.

2. Add 6 cups of the water and the tomato, carrot, corn, beans, salt, cumin, oregano, thyme, and sugar. Bring to a boil, reduce the heat to low, cover, and simmer for 40 to 60 minutes, stirring every 10 minutes or so.

3. Place the remaining 1 cup water in a blender with the chipotle, adobo, and flour and blend until a smooth paste forms. Increase the heat to high, and when the soup boils, add the paste to the soup, stirring constantly to make sure no lumps form. Remove from the heat, add the cheese and olives, and stir until the cheese is completely melted. Ladle into bowls and serve.

Tips/Variations

Garnish possibilities: Corn chips, cilantro, lime wedges, guacamole, and/or sour cream.

> **Hands-on prep time:** 15 minutes
> **Cook time:** 1 hour 10 minutes
> **Total time:** 1 hour 15 minutes
> **Makes** about 14 cups

Ingredients

- 2 Tbsp oil
- 1 cup diced onion
- 1 Tbsp minced garlic (2-3 cloves)
- 1 cup chopped celery (2 stalks)
- 1 cup chopped green bell pepper
- 7 cups water
- One 28-ounce can diced tomato (or 3½ cups fresh)
- 1 cup chopped carrot (1-2 carrots)
- 1 cup frozen corn
- 3½ cups cooked or canned black beans (rinsed and drained)
- 1 Tbsp salt or to taste
- 1 Tbsp ground cumin
- 1 Tbsp dried oregano
- 1 tsp dried thyme
- 1 Tbsp sugar
- 1-2 finely minced canned chipotle peppers plus 1 Tbsp adobo sauce
- ½ cup unbleached white flour
- 4 cups grated cheddar cheese (1 pound)
- ¾ cup pitted, sliced black olives (3 ounces)

October Harvest

Savor the sweetness and smooth-yet-hearty texture of delectable winter squash with this simple recipe. With warm bread it makes a great autumn meal, though it's also a perfect prelude to any holiday dinner. Both kids and parents will look forward to it.

Procedure

1. Heat the ghee, butter, or oil in a 5-quart pot over high heat. Add the onion and sauté for a couple of minutes until it begins to brown.

2. Add the water, squash, sugar, salt, coriander, nutmeg, allspice, and turmeric and bring to a boil. Reduce the heat to medium, cover, and simmer for about 15 minutes until the squash is tender.

3. Meanwhile, prepare the garnish (optional). To do so, preheat the oven to broil. Spread the breads on a baking tray and place a slice of cheese on top of each. Broil for a minute or two until the cheese is melted. Remove from the oven and slice each piece into 4 wedges.

4. Add the half-and-half and garlic to the soup and simmer gently for a few more minutes. Place 4 cups soup in a blender and blend until smooth. Return to the pot and stir through. Ladle into bowls, garnish with the Cheese Toasts (optional), and serve.

Hands-on prep time: 15 minutes
Cook time: 25 minutes
Total time: 40 minutes
Makes about 10 cups

Ingredients

2 Tbsp ghee, butter, or oil
1 cup slivered onion
4 cups water
9 cups cubed butternut or kabocha squash (3½ pounds)
1 Tbsp brown sugar or to taste
2½ tsp salt or to taste
1 tsp ground coriander
½ tsp nutmeg
½ tsp allspice
¼ tsp turmeric
2 cups half-and-half (cream)
1 Tbsp minced garlic (2-3 cloves)

Cheese Toast Garnish (optional)

6-8 whole wheat mini pita breads (or other bread)
Slices of cheddar or other favorite cheese

Tutti Frutti

This tropical soup makes a fun brunch item or refreshing dessert. You can vary the fruits according to season and availability—there really are no hard and fast rules as long as you've got delicious, juicy fruit. I've served it a few times for baby and toddler birthday parties, and it's always a hit.

Plan ahead: Remember to peel your bananas and put them in the freezer the night before. Do the same for the mangoes if you want them frozen and are using fresh. Chill all your other ingredients in advance so you can eat this soup right away.

Procedure

In batches, place the juice, coconut milk, bananas, and mango in a blender and blend until smooth. Pour into a 3-quart bowl and add the pineapple tidbits, the lychees or grapes, and half of the kiwifruit and stir through. Ladle into bowls, garnish with the remaining kiwifruit, the berries, and the starfruit (optional), and serve immediately.

Tips/Variations

Sweetening tip: If your fruit isn't that sweet, add sugar, honey, or maple syrup to taste.

Leftovers: Make Tutti Frutti popsicles.

> **Hands-on prep time:** 30 minutes
> **Total time:** 30 minutes
> **Makes** about 8 cups

Ingredients

- 2 cups chilled pineapple juice
- 1 cup coconut milk
- 3 frozen bananas, roughly chopped
- 3 cups chilled or frozen mango, roughly chopped (2-3 large mangos)
- ½ cup pineapple tidbits (preferably fresh, but canned will do)
- 1 dozen lychees (peeled, pitted, and quartered) or 2 dozen grapes (halved)
- 2 kiwifruit, peeled and sliced into half moons
- 1 cup whole raspberries, pitted cherries, or sliced strawberries
- 1 starfruit, sliced ¼ inch thick (optional)

Gourmet

If you're in the mood for something dramatically different *and* doable, you'll find these enticing recipes will make you look like a gourmet.

Curried Apple Squash Soup

Elegant and cozy, this savory-sweet curry soup will make guests feel warm and welcome at your table. The candied nuts add a nice contrast in both taste and texture. Make them a few hours or a day in advance if you like (but hide them well, as they've been known to mysteriously disappear!). You can also use plain toasted nuts instead.

The best approach to making this recipe: Prepare the Candied Nut garnish first (p. 171), then make the soup and caramelized onion at the same time.

Procedure

1. Cut the squash in half, remove the seeds, and slice each half into 4 pieces. Steam the squash for 25 minutes. Add the apple and steam for another 10 minutes or until everything is tender. Remove from the heat and set aside for about 15 minutes until the squash is cool enough to handle, reserving the steaming water for part of the 4-cup measurement. Scoop out the flesh and discard the skin.

2. In batches, place the squash, apple, and water in a blender and blend until smooth. Pour into a 4-quart pot and stir in ½ teaspoon of the salt, the curry paste, and the sugar. Let the soup simmer uncovered over low heat for 15 to 20 minutes.

3. Meanwhile, heat ½ tablespoon of the oil, butter, or ghee in a small skillet over high heat. Add the fennel seeds and sauté for a few seconds until they darken, then add them immediately to the soup.

4. In the same skillet, heat the remaining tablespoon of oil, butter, or ghee over medium-high heat. Add the onion and remaining ¼ teaspoon salt and sauté for about 15 minutes until the onion softens, browns, and caramelizes.

5. Ladle the soup into bowls, garnish with the sautéed onion and nuts, and serve.

> **Hands-on prep time:** 30 minutes
> **Cook time:** 1 hour 5 minutes
> **Total time:** 1 hour 20 minutes (including cooling time for squash)
> **Makes** about 8 cups

Ingredients

- 3¼ **pounds kabocha or butternut squash**
- 2 **cups peeled, chopped sweet apple** (like fuji or braeburn) (2 apples)
- 4 **cups water**
- ¾ **tsp salt or to taste**
- 1½ **tsp Patak's Original Mild Curry Paste** (or madras curry powder)
- 2 **tsp sugar or to taste**
- 1½ **Tbsp oil, butter, or ghee**
- 1 **tsp fennel seeds**
- 1½ **cups finely slivered vidalia or other sweet onion** for garnishing
- **Candied Nuts** (p. 171) for garnishing

Candied Nuts

Ingredients

2 cups walnuts or pecans, chopped
½ cup raw or granulated sugar
¼ tsp ground cinnamon
2 Tbsp water

Procedure

1. Preheat the oven to 350°F.

2. Spread the nuts on a cookie sheet and bake for 10 minutes, stirring once halfway. Allow to cool.

3. Combine the sugar, cinnamon, and water in a small saucepan and melt the sugar over low heat. When the sugar is dissolved, add the nuts and increase the heat to medium-high. Stir constantly until the syrup crystallizes, about 2 to 3 minutes. Immediately transfer back to the same cookie sheet and break up any clumps of nuts. Cool for a few minutes before using.

Wonderful Walnuts
Rich in omega 3 fatty acids, B vitamins, and magnesium, delicious walnuts can help reduce pain and inflammation in the body. According to Chinese medicine, they also warm your body and nourish your brain, kidneys, and adrenal glands. Always be sure to buy the freshest walnuts you can find as they become rancid quite easily.

Szechwan Dumpling Soup

Everyone I know loves dumplings—though few dare to make them. If you'd like to try, this recipe is a good way to start as it calls for half-moon dumplings, which are definitely the easiest shape to make. Sweet and savory, this mouthwatering soup appeals to tastebuds of all ages.

Procedure

1. Heat the oil in a 4-quart pot over medium-high heat. Add the onion, garlic, and mushrooms and sauté for a few minutes until they begin to brown.

2. Add the water or broth, bouillon cubes (if using water), peanut butter, soy sauce, vinegar, and sugar. Increase the heat to high and bring to a boil. Reduce the heat to low, cover, and simmer as you prepare the dumplings (see next page).

3. Raise the heat to high and give the soup a stir. Add a little more water if you need to and salt to taste. Gently bring the soup to a quick boil, add the dumplings, reduce the heat to medium, cover, and simmer for about 5 minutes, stirring every minute.

4. Remove from the heat and add the cucumber, sprouts, and chili and stir through. Ladle into bowls, garnish with peanuts and cilantro or mint, and serve.

Tips/Variations

Spice it up: Szechwan cooking is known for its spiciness, so if you like it really hot, add a teaspoon of Chinese chili paste or chili garlic paste. You can even stir in a tablespoon of your favorite Thai curry paste.

Serve with steamed rice or a cool noodle salad.

> **Hands-on prep time:** 35 minutes
> **Cook time:** 25 minutes
> **Total time:** 45 minutes
> Makes about 8 cups

Ingredients

- ¼ cup toasted sesame oil
- 1 cup chopped onion
- 1 Tbsp minced garlic (2-3 cloves)
- 4 cups finely sliced shiitake mushrooms (stems removed, 1 pound)
- 7½ cups water or Basic Veggie Broth (p. 282)
- 2 veggie bouillon cubes (only if using water)
- ¾-1 cup unsalted peanut butter
- ⅓ cup soy sauce or to taste
- 2 Tbsp rice vinegar
- 2 Tbsp sugar
- Salt to taste
- ⅔ cup peeled, sliced cucumber
- 2 cups chopped bean sprouts
- 1 tsp minced fresh chili or red chili flakes
- ¼ cup chopped roasted unsalted peanuts for garnishing
- Minced or whole cilantro or mint leaves for garnishing
- 1 recipe Szechwan Dumplings (p. 174)

Delicious, Nutritious Shiitake Mushrooms
I eat shiitake mushrooms nearly every day, not only for their distinct and robust flavor, but also for their many impressive health benefits. Prized in Asia for thousands of years for promoting longevity, the shiitake stimulates the immune system to fight against everything from the common cold to cancer. Studies have also shown it effective in lowering bad cholesterol. A good source of iron, protein, fiber, calcium, B vitamins, and vitamin C, the shiitake can be found fresh in most grocery stores.

Szechwan Dumplings

Ingredients

⅔ cup crumbled firm tofu
⅓ cup minced celery
2 tsp minced ginger
2 Tbsp minced cilantro or mint leaves
½ tsp salt
2 Tbsp water
2 Tbsp cornstarch
16 eggless wonton wrappers*

Procedure

1. To make the filling, combine the tofu, celery, ginger, cilantro or mint, and salt in a 2-quart bowl.

2. To assemble the dumplings, combine the water and cornstarch to form a smooth paste. Use your index finger to moisten the edges of the wonton wrappers with the paste. Place 1 teaspoon of filling in the center of each wrapper, then fold the wrapper in half over the filling. Press the edges of each wrapper firmly together until the dumpling is sealed.

*Eggless wonton wrappers can be found in some regular grocery stores and in Chinatown.

Cauliflower Tomato Soup
with Fresh Panir

Making panir, or fresh cheese, is a ritual I've grown to love. It's both relaxing and rewarding to stir the milk and watch the curd magically separate from the whey. When you taste it pan-fried to perfection and added to this sumptuous curried cauliflower soup, you'll definitely agree it's worth a little patience! The soup itself is very straightforward and simple to make. It goes well with basmati rice and samosas or pakoras.

Plan ahead: Make the panir at least 5 hours before you intend to serve the soup.

The best approach to making this recipe: Once the panir has firmed up for 4 hours, begin making the soup (see next page). While the soup simmers, pan-fry the curd to add at the end.

Procedure

Panir

1. Place the milk in a 6-quart pot over high heat and bring to a boil, stirring constantly. Once it boils, immediately add the yogurt and return to a boil. The milk will separate into curds and whey. Remove from the heat immediately.

2. Place a fine sieve over a large bowl and carefully pour or ladle the curds into the sieve, catching the whey in the bowl below. Transfer the whey to another container, reserve for the soup, and replace the bowl underneath the strainer. Rest a plate directly on top of the curd and place about 5 pounds of weight on the plate. Let the curd sit like this for 4 hours to firm up, then cut it into bite-size cubes.

3. Place the oil or ghee in a large skillet over high heat, add the curd, sprinkle with the salt, and pan-fry for 5 to 10 minutes, stirring occasionally, until golden and crisp at the edges. Set aside.

> Hands-on prep time: 50 minutes
> Cook time: 50 minutes
> Total time: 1 hour 10 minutes (not including panir firming time)
> Panir firming time: 4 hours
> Makes about 10 cups

Ingredients
Panir
½ **gallon whole milk (8 cups)**
2 cups regular or low-fat plain yogurt
1 Tbsp oil or ghee
¼ tsp salt or to taste

Ingredients

1 Tbsp oil or ghee

½ cup slivered onion

2 tsp minced garlic (2 cloves)

1 tsp cumin seeds

½ tsp black mustard seeds

One 28-ounce can diced tomato (or 3½ cups fresh)

4-5 cups bite-size cauliflower florets

4 cups reserved whey or water

1 Tbsp minced ginger

2 Tbsp sugar

1 tsp ground coriander

¼ tsp whole black peppercorns

⅛ tsp turmeric

2½ tsp salt or to taste

1 tsp minced fresh chili or red chili flakes (optional)

¼ cup minced fresh Italian parsley, mint, or cilantro

Soup

Procedure

1. Heat the oil or ghee in a 5-quart pot over medium-high heat. Add the onion and garlic and sauté for a couple of minutes until they begin to brown. Add the cumin and mustard seeds and sauté for another 30 seconds.

2. Add the tomato, cauliflower, whey or water, ginger, sugar, coriander, peppercorns, turmeric, and salt. Cover, increase the heat to high, and bring to a boil. Reduce the heat to medium and simmer for 10 to 15 minutes until the cauliflower is tender.

3. Add the chili (optional), fresh herbs, and pan-fried curd, simmer for another couple of minutes, then remove from the heat and serve.

Tips/Variations

Whey is the way: Whey makes for a fuller-flavored and slightly tangier soup. I highly recommend it over water.

Tofu shortcut: Omit the panir and pan-fry cubes of tofu instead.

Soupe de Seitan l'Orange

A few of my friends insist this spectacular Szechwan-inspired soup is really from heaven. Sumptuous chunks of caramelized Seitan l'Orange sit atop a sesame-flavored vegetable-shiitake broth and a nest of crispy rice noodles. Served with salad-stuffed summer rolls, it's easily a main course. If you're not up for frying the noodles, simply add them to the soup (dry) and let them soften a few minutes before serving.

Plan ahead: This recipe calls for Asian Broth (p. 282).

Procedure

1. Heat the sesame oil in a 6-quart pot over high heat. Add the onion and sauté for a few minutes until it begins to brown. Add the chili, garlic, mushrooms, and carrot and sauté for a couple of more minutes.

2. Add the broth, water chestnuts, and bok choy, cover, and bring to a boil. Reduce the heat to medium-low, cover, and simmer as you prepare the seitan and noodles.

3. For the noodles, heat 1 inch of oil in a medium pot over high heat. Test if the oil is hot enough by dropping in one dry noodle; if it immediately puffs up, then the oil is ready for frying. When the oil is hot enough, place the noodles (in small batches) in the oil, turning over immediately with tongs. Within a couple of seconds, remove the noodles from the oil and set aside to drain on paper towels. The noodles should sizzle and become crispy and light, like puffed rice. They should also remain white (with perhaps a few beige spots). Be careful as the oil may sputter.

4. Ladle the soup into shallow bowls and let it cool for a few minutes. When the soup is just cool enough to eat, add a nest of noodles and top the noodles with the seitan and green onions. Serve immediately before the noodles become soggy.

Hands-on prep time: 30 minutes
Cook time: 50 minutes (not including Asian Broth time)
Total time: 50 minutes
Makes about 12 cups soup plus seitan and noodles

Ingredients

2 Tbsp toasted sesame oil
½ cup slivered onion
1 split fresh chili (stem removed)
1 Tbsp minced garlic (2-3 cloves)
1 cup sliced shiitake mushrooms (stems removed)
1 cup julienned or chopped carrot (1-2 carrots)
12 cups Asian Broth (p. 282)
¼ cup sliced water chestnuts, slivered
2 cups chopped baby bok choy
1 recipe Seitan l'Orange (p. 292)
Oil for frying
4 ounces dried rice vermicelli
¼ cup minced green onion (4-5 onions) for garnishing

Waldorf Chowder

with Brie & Pear Chutney

I love it when my friend Christine comes to visit. An artful vegetarian chef, she always takes our breath away with something beautiful and unique. This recipe is a perfect example. Although impressive, it's actually very easy to make. I consider it gourmet only because it will make you look like one.

Procedure

1. Heat the oil in a 6-quart pot over high heat. Add the celery and leek and sauté for a few minutes until they begin to brown. Add the caraway seeds and sauté for another minute.

2. Add 5 cups of the water or broth, the bouillon cube(s) (if using water), potato, fresh herbs, mustard, salt, and pepper and bring to a boil. Reduce the heat to medium, cover, and simmer for 15 minutes or until the potato is tender. Meanwhile, begin preparing the chutney.

3. Combine the remaining 1 cup water or broth with the flour until a smooth paste forms. Add this to the soup gradually, stirring constantly to prevent lumps from forming. Add the cream, increase the heat to high, and gently bring to just under a boil. Remove from the heat, add the garlic, and stir through. Ladle the soup into bowls and garnish with brie and chutney.

Hands-on prep time: 25 minutes
Cook time: 30 minutes
Total time: 45 minutes
Makes about 12 cups

Ingredients

2 Tbsp oil

2½ cups diced celery (4 stalks)

1½ cups finely sliced leek (2 leeks)

1 tsp caraway seeds

6 cups water or Basic Veggie Broth (p. 282)

1-2 veggie bouillon cubes (only if using water)

6 cups cubed red potato (4-6 potatoes)

1-2 sprigs fresh thyme, chervil, tarragon, or rosemary

2 Tbsp dijon mustard

1 Tbsp salt or to taste

Fresh ground black pepper to taste

½ cup unbleached white flour

2 cups half-and-half (cream)

1 Tbsp minced garlic (2-3 cloves)

One 8-ounce brie wheel (room temperature), cut into 6-12 wedges for garnishing

1 recipe Pear Chutney for garnishing (p. 295)

Healing

If you have a health condition or feel you may be predisposed to one, these tasty, nourishing recipes can provide nutritional support as you travel the road to better health.

Cream of Summer Harvest

Antioxidant Action

This delicious healing soup is filled with aromatic delights like fennel, tarragon, asparagus, and parsley to help detoxify and fortify your body. Raw almonds create a creamy, dairy-free foundation for antioxidant-packed foods that fight disease by destroying or removing cancer-causing free radicals. Blend half the soup if you prefer a thicker consistency.

Plan ahead: Soak the almonds in 3 cups of water at room temperature for 8 to 12 hours. This lets the nuts germinate, enlivening them so they're more nutritious (and less fattening).

Procedure

1. Strain and rinse the soaked almonds, discarding the soaking water. Place the almonds and fresh water in a blender and blend until smooth, in batches if necessary.

2. Heat the oil or ghee in a 3-quart pot over high heat. Add the cauliflower or broccoli, fennel, carrot, celery, onion, and ¼ teaspoon of the salt and sauté for 1 minute. Cover and cook for another few minutes until the onion begins to brown, stirring occasionally.

3. Add the blended almond milk, remaining teaspoon salt, tarragon, mustard, and turmeric and bring to just under a boil. Reduce the heat to low, cover, and simmer for about 5 minutes.

4. Add the asparagus, tomatoes, and parsley, increase the heat to medium-high, cover, and simmer for about 5 minutes until the asparagus is tender. Remove from the heat, ladle into bowls, garnish with parsley, and serve.

Soak time: 8-12 hours
Hands-on prep time: 15 minutes
Cook time: 15 minutes
Total time: 30 minutes (not including soak time)
Makes about 6 cups

Ingredients

1 cup raw almonds, soaked*

4 cups water

1 Tbsp oil or ghee

1 cup bite-size cauliflower or broccoli florets

1 cup slivered fennel

1 cup finely chopped carrot (1-2 carrots)

¼ cup diced celery

¼ cup minced onion

1¼ tsp salt or to taste

1½ tsp minced fresh tarragon (or ½ tsp dried)

1 tsp dry mustard

¼ tsp turmeric

1 cup chopped asparagus (leave tips whole)

½ cup whole grape tomatoes

½ cup minced parsley
plus extra for garnishing

*The almonds will expand to about 1½ cups after soaking. Use all 1½ cups.

Red Vegetable Power

Antioxidant Action

Curl up in a cozy chair with a mug of this soup and feel warmed and strengthened from the inside out. Rich with powerful phytonutrients that lend intense deep red pigments, this simple, easy-to-make soup is great to "fast" on when you're feeling run down. Antioxidants in cabbage, beet, carrot, leek, apricot, turmeric, miso, and rosemary help keep cold and flu bugs at bay as they work on a cellular level to fight more serious health threats like cancer and heart disease.

Procedure

1. Heat the oil or ghee in a 3-quart pot over high heat. Add the leek and sauté for a few minutes until it just begins to brown.

2. Add the water, beet, carrot, apricot, cayenne, turmeric, and Braggs or tamari. Bring to a boil, reduce the heat to medium, cover, and simmer for 10 minutes. Add the rosemary and cabbage and simmer for another 5 minutes or until the cabbage completely wilts.

3. Remove from the heat. Ladle ⅓ cup of the broth into a cup and combine with the miso until smooth. Add this to the soup along with the vinegar and parsley and stir through. Ladle into bowls and serve.

> **Hands-on prep time:** 15 minutes
> **Cook time:** 20 minutes
> **Total time:** 30 minutes
> **Makes** about 5 cups

Ingredients

1 tsp oil or ghee

1 cup finely sliced leek
(1-2 leeks)

4 cups water

1 cup diced beet

½ cup chopped carrot

1 rounded Tbsp minced dried apricot

¼ tsp cayenne pepper

Pinch of turmeric

3 Tbsp Bragg Liquid Aminos or tamari or to taste

1 tsp minced fresh rosemary

1½ cups finely shredded red or green cabbage

1-2 Tbsp miso of choice

1-2 Tbsp apple cider vinegar

½ cup minced Italian parsley

Easy Veggie Bean Soup

Balance Blood Sugar

This is definitely what I call a low-maintenance soup. Flavorful, wholesome, and quick to make, it's something you can feel good about feeding your family. Green beans, parsnip, tomato, parsley, and kohlrabi bring in fresh body-balancing nutrition, while tender— almost creamy—pinto beans lend body and heartiness.

Procedure

1. Place the water, beans, parsnip, tomato, kohlrabi (or turnip or rutabaga), salt, and garlic in a 3-quart pot and bring to a boil over high heat. Reduce the heat to medium, cover, and simmer for 15 minutes or until the veggies are tender. Add the green beans and parsley and simmer for another 5 to 10 minutes.

2. Either add the Braggs or tamari or, if using miso, ladle ⅓ cup of the broth into a cup and combine with the miso until smooth, then add this to the soup. Stir in the nutritional yeast, ladle into bowls, garnish with parsley, and serve.

Tips/Variations

Blended variation: To thicken it up, blend half the soup.

Serve with Quinoa Pilaf (p. 290) for an easy, nourishing meal.

Hands-on prep time: 10 minutes
Cook time: 25 minutes
Total time: 30 minutes
Makes about 6 cups

Ingredients

4½ cups water

2 cups cooked or canned pinto beans (rinsed and drained)

1 cup chopped parsnip (1-2 parsnips)

½ cup chopped tomato

1 cup chopped kohlrabi, turnip, or rutabaga

1 tsp salt or to taste

1½ tsp minced garlic (1-2 cloves)

½ cup chopped green beans, fresh or frozen

2-3 Tbsp minced Italian parsley plus extra for garnishing

2 Tbsp Bragg Liquid Aminos, tamari, or miso of choice

2 Tbsp nutritional yeast

Butternut Lentil Soup

Balance Blood Sugar

This tasty homestyle favorite appeals to all ages and has often been rated a 10 on the deliciousness scale by my son and his friends. No one, in fact, will even guess it's a healing soup. It combines gentle butternut squash, lentils, broccoli, and mushrooms to create a blood-sugar-regulating soup that's simple enough to make every day.

Procedure

1. Place the water and lentils in a 3-quart pot over high heat. Bring to a boil, reduce the heat to medium, cover, and simmer for 20 minutes. Add the tomato, squash, lemon pepper, and ¼ cup Braggs or tamari, then cover and cook for 10 minutes. Add the broccoli and simmer for another 5 to 10 minutes.

2. Meanwhile, heat the oil in a medium skillet over high heat. Add the leek, mushrooms, and remaining 1 teaspoon Braggs or tamari and sauté for a few minutes until the mushrooms brown. Add the garlic, sauté for another minute, and remove from the heat. Add this to the soup and stir through. Ladle into bowls and serve.

Tips/Variations

Veggie variation: You can use yucca instead of squash or half yucca, half squash—especially if you're doubling the recipe (which I often do). Yucca takes a bit longer to cook, so add it to the soup after the lentils have cooked for 10 minutes.

Cinnamon variation: You can increase the blood-sugar-balancing properties of this soup by adding ¼ teaspoon cinnamon.

> **Hands-on prep time:** 15 minutes
> **Cook time:** 40 minutes
> **Total time:** 45 minutes
> **Makes** about 6 cups

Ingredients

- 5 cups water
- ½ cup dried brown lentils, sifted and rinsed well
- ½ cup chopped tomato
- 1½ cups cubed butternut squash
- 1 tsp lemon pepper or to taste
- ¼ cup plus 1 tsp Bragg Liquid Aminos or tamari or to taste
- 1½ cups chopped broccoli
- 1 tsp oil
- 1 cup finely sliced leek (1-2 leeks)
- 1 cup sliced cremini or button mushrooms
- 1 tsp minced garlic

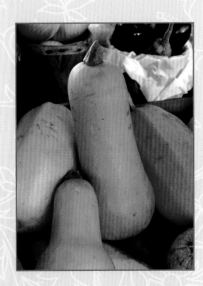

Parsnip Apple Bisque

Beautiful Skin

I like to make this savory, low-fat soup in the fall when local parsnips and apples are fresh and plentiful. Celery, apple, and nutty parsnip roots are rich sources of silicon, a trace mineral needed for skin elasticity, while cabbage is rich in sulfur—also known as the beauty mineral. Creamy navy beans also help nourish and beautify your skin.

Procedure

1. Place all the ingredients except the tahini or mayonnaise in a 3-quart pot and bring to a boil over high heat. Cover, reduce the heat to medium, and cook for 10 to 15 minutes until the parsnip is tender.

2. Meanwhile, prepare the garnish. To do so, heat the oil in a medium skillet over high heat. Add the remaining ingredients and sauté for a few minutes until the cabbage is just tender. Do not overcook or the cabbage will lose its vibrant color.

3. In batches, place the soup in a blender with the tahini or mayonnaise and blend until smooth. Add a little extra water if necessary and adjust the salt if needed. Pour the soup into bowls, garnish with the sautéed cabbage, and serve.

> **Hands-on prep time:** 20 minutes
> **Cook time:** 25 minutes
> **Total time:** 35 minutes
> **Makes** about 6 cups plus 1 cup cabbage

Ingredients

- 3 cups water
- 2 cups chopped parsnip (3-5 parsnips)
- 1 cup cooked or canned navy or great northern beans (rinsed and drained)
- 1 cup chopped celery (2 stalks)
- 1 cup peeled, chopped sweet-tart apple (like Granny Smith)
- 1½ Tbsp minced ginger
- ¼ cup chopped Italian parsley (loosely packed)
- 1½ tsp salt or to taste
- 1 Tbsp prepared horseradish
- 1 heaping Tbsp tahini or eggless mayonnaise

Sautéed Cabbage Garnish

- 1½ tsp oil
- 2 cups slivered red cabbage
- 2 Tbsp chopped chives
- ¼ tsp salt
- 3 Tbsp finely sliced dried apricot (optional)

Olive Avocado Cream

Beautiful Skin

This 5-minute soup has a rich flavor and a wonderful silken texture that comes from a blend of sumptuous olives, ripe avocado, and baby lima beans. Abundant with valuable antioxidants like vitamins A and E, this beauty soup helps moisturize and protect your skin on the deepest levels. By nourishing dry, depleted cells, these nutrients help revive your skin, restore elasticity, and promote a smooth, creamy complexion. Cucumber and lemon are also well known for their innate abilities to promote a radiant, healthy glow.

Plan ahead: If using frozen baby lima beans, you will need to cook then cool them first, which takes an additional twenty minutes.

Procedure

Place all the ingredients except the garnishes in a blender and blend until smooth. Pour into bowls, garnish with bell pepper, dill, and cucumber, and serve.

Tips/Variations

Serve with a simple green salad or slices of green apple as a light summer lunch.

Total time: 5 minutes
Makes about 4 cups

Ingredients

1 cup cooked or canned baby lima beans* or broad beans

¼ cup pitted green olives

½ cup avocado

2½ cups cold water

½ cup chopped red bell pepper
plus extra minced for garnishing

2 tsp minced fresh dill
plus extra for garnishing

2 tsp lemon juice

1 tsp honey

¾ tsp Spike or to taste

¼ cup finely diced cucumber
for garnishing

*If using frozen beans, boil them first. Bring 2 cups water to a boil over high heat and add the beans. Reduce heat to medium-low, cover, and simmer for 15 minutes. Remove from heat, strain, and rinse under cold water until cool.

Carrot Leek Bisque

Breathe Easy

In addition to my yoga breathing practice, I try to take care of my lungs through my diet as well. For example, this flavorful, elegant recipe is a wonderful lung tonic and purifier. Nearly all the ingredients possess some inherent power to protect these vital organs from infection, congestion, weakness, and disease. Horseradish and rosemary are especially beneficial to the lungs.

Procedure

1. Heat the oil in a 3-quart pot over high heat. Add the leek and sauté for a couple of minutes until it begins to brown. Add the remaining ingredients except the pine nuts. Bring to a boil, reduce the heat to medium, cover, and simmer for 10 minutes or until the carrots are tender.

2. Meanwhile, prepare the garnish. To do so, heat the oil in a small skillet over high heat. Add the garlic and sauté for about 15 seconds. Add the kale and salt and cook for a few minutes until the kale is wilted.

3. Place the soup in a blender and blend until smooth. Return to the pot. Ladle into bowls, garnish with the wilted kale and pine nuts, and serve.

Tips/Variations

Flavor tip: If your carrots aren't that sweet or flavorful, add a veggie bouillon cube and honey to taste.

Serve with a Smoky Tempeh (p. 291) sandwich as a tasty lunch during flu season.

> Hands-on prep time: 15 minutes
> Cook time: 15 minutes
> Total time: 30 minutes
> Makes about 5 cups

Ingredients

1 tsp oil

¾ cup finely sliced leek

4 cups water

3 cups chopped carrot
(4-6 carrots)

2 Tbsp minced dried apricot

1 Tbsp prepared or fresh-grated horseradish

1½ Tbsp Spike or to taste

1 tsp minced fresh rosemary
(or ½ tsp dried)

2 Tbsp toasted pine nuts*
for garnishing

Wilted Kale Garnish

1 tsp oil

½ tsp minced garlic

1 cup finely chopped kale
(packed)

⅛ tsp salt

*See Toasting Nuts and Seeds, p. 10.

Spicy Lotus Root Soup

Breathe Easy

Light, brothy, and beautiful, this truly Asian soup helps clear, strengthen, and protect your lungs. The pungent daikon radish contains natural decongestants and stimulates the lung meridian, bringing chi energy to the chest. Pineapple possesses the natural anti-inflammatory enzyme bromelain, which helps relieve bronchitis and sore throats.

Procedure

1. Place all the ingredients except the bok choy and pineapple in a 3-quart pot over high heat. Bring to a boil, reduce the heat to medium, cover, and simmer for 10 minutes.

2. Add the bok choy and pineapple (optional) and simmer for another 5 to 10 minutes or until all the veggies are tender. Remove from the heat, ladle into bowls, and serve.

Tips/Variations

Make it a meal: Add a small bundle of bean thread noodles (a.k.a. glass or mung noodles) in Step 2. Let them soften for a few minutes before serving. Increase the water slightly and salt to taste.

Garnish possibilities: Chopped bean sprouts and cilantro.

Hands-on prep time: 15 minutes
Cook time: 25 minutes
Total time: 30 minutes
Makes about 6 cups

Ingredients

- 4 cups water
- 1½ cups cubed butternut squash
- ½ cup peeled, thinly sliced lotus root (10-12 rounds)
- 1 Tbsp minced ginger
- ¼ cup peeled, finely diced daikon radish
- ½ cup finely cubed firm silken tofu
- Dash of white pepper
- ½ tsp minced fresh chili or red chili flakes
- ¼ cup Bragg Liquid Aminos or tamari or to taste
- 2 cups sliced baby bok choy
- 2 rounded Tbsp finely diced pineapple (optional)

Napa Mushroom Soup

Detoxify Your Body

This energizing, protein-rich soup draws its cleansing powers from shiitake and oyster mushrooms and burdock root, which help the body eliminate toxins. Burdock, also known as gobo, is an excellent vegetable for detoxifying the blood and liver. If you can't find it, try using turnip or rutabaga instead. This soup also helps boost immunity, regulate blood sugar, and promote weight loss.

Procedure

1. Place the water, burdock, seaweed, and star anise in a 3-quart pot over high heat. Bring to a boil, reduce the heat to medium, cover, and simmer for about 15 minutes until the burdock is tender.

2. Meanwhile, heat the oil in a medium skillet over medium heat. Add the shiitake and oyster mushrooms, leek, garlic, sesame seeds, and Braggs or tamari and sauté for a few minutes until the mushroom and leek begin to brown. Set aside.

3. Once the burdock is tender, increase the heat to high, add the cabbage to the soup, and bring to a boil. Remove from the heat and add the sautéed mushrooms and leek, reserving some for garnishing (optional).

4. Ladle ⅛ cup of the broth into a cup and combine with the miso until smooth. Add this to the soup along with the vinegar and stir through. Ladle into bowls, top with the sautéed mushrooms and leek and the radish (both optional), and serve.

> **Hands-on prep time:** 20 minutes
> **Cook time:** 30 minutes
> **Total time:** 30 minutes
> **Makes** about 5 cups

Ingredients

5 cups water

1½ cups peeled, finely chopped burdock root* (gobo)

1 tsp hijiki or arame seaweed

1 star anise

2¼ tsp toasted sesame oil

1½ cups finely sliced shiitake mushrooms (stems removed)

½ cup sliced or torn oyster mushrooms

¾ cup finely sliced leek

1½ tsp minced garlic (1-2 cloves)

1 tsp sesame seeds

1 Tbsp Bragg Liquid Aminos or tamari or to taste

3 cups shredded napa cabbage

3 Tbsp light miso

1 Tbsp apple cider vinegar

2 Tbsp minced red radish
for garnishing (optional)

*Burdock root is an interesting root vegetable that usually arrives at the market when about 3 feet long. It is dark brown, woody-looking, and narrow like a carrot.

Spring Detox

Detoxify Your Body

Fresh, cleansing, and enlivening, this is the perfect recipe for spring, a time characterized by renewal, purity, and energy. Ingredients like beet, asparagus, parsley, and miso help your body eliminate long-stored toxins, promoting a revival of health. You can almost taste this soup rejuvenating your body.

Procedure

1. Heat the oil in a 2-quart pot over high heat. Add the onion and sauté for a couple of minutes until it begins to brown. Add the celery and sauté for another minute.

2. Add the water, beet, carrot, and ginger and bring to a boil. Reduce the heat to medium, cover, and simmer for 15 minutes. Add the asparagus and parsley and simmer for another 5 minutes or so, then remove from the heat.

3. Ladle ⅓ cup of the broth into a cup and combine with the miso until smooth. Add this to the soup. Salt to taste if necessary, ladle into bowls, and serve.

Tips/Variations

Broth variation: Cook the soup for an hour, then strain the vegetables. Add the miso to the broth. This is a wonderful formula for fasting.

Tangy variation: Add a splash of apple cider vinegar or reduce the miso by half and add ¾ teaspoon umeboshi plum paste for a slightly more intense cleansing action.

> **Hands-on prep time:** 15 minutes
> **Cook time:** 30 minutes
> **Total time:** 35 minutes
> **Makes** about 4 cups

Ingredients

- 1 tsp oil
- ¼ cup diced onion
- ½ cup chopped celery
- 4 cups water
- 1½ cups cubed beet
- ½ cup chopped carrot
- 1 Tbsp minced ginger
- 1 cup chopped asparagus
  (bases trimmed, tips left whole)
- ¼ cup minced Italian parsley
- 3 Tbsp miso of choice
- Salt to taste

Red Lentil Sauerkraut Soup

Heart-healthy ingredients like garlic, celery, red lentils, turmeric, and sauerkraut support your circulation, immune function, digestion, elimination, and assimilation of nutrients. If you're a fan of sauerkraut, you'll love this recipe.

Procedure

1. Heat the oil in a 3-quart pot over high heat. Add the onions and sauté for a few minutes until they begin to brown. Add the celery and garlic and sauté for another minute or until they begin to brown. Add the caraway seeds and sauté for 30 seconds more.

2. Add the remaining ingredients except the sauerkraut. Bring to a boil, reduce the heat to medium, cover, and simmer for 15 to 20 minutes or until the turnip or rutabaga is tender and the lentils have lost their form. Add the sauerkraut and simmer for another minute, then remove from the heat. Ladle into bowls and serve.

Tips/Variations

Sauerkraut tip: A good-quality sauerkraut should contain nothing but a little bit of salt and cabbage. No vinegar!

Make it a meal: Top or serve with Seasoned TVP Nuggets (p. 293). Complement with brown rice.

Hands-on prep time: 10 minutes
Cook time: 25 minutes
Total time: 35 minutes
Makes about 6 cups

Ingredients

1 tsp oil

8 pearl onions,* peeled and trimmed (or ½ cup diced onion)

¾ cup diced celery (2 stalks)

1 tsp minced garlic

¼ tsp caraway seeds

4 cups water

⅔ cup red lentils (sifted and rinsed)

½ cup chopped carrot

1 cup diced turnip or rutabaga

½ cup peeled, diced sweet-tart apple (like Granny Smith)

2 Tbsp miso of choice or 1 tsp salt or to taste

1-2 Tbsp nutritional yeast

Dash of turmeric

1 bay leaf

1 cup sauerkraut

*You can easily remove the pearl onion skins by blanching them first (see p. 16).

Valentine Soup

Asian healers have long believed red vegetables and legumes to support the heart, not only because of the nutrients they contain, but also because of a subtle influence on the blood and circulation. Hearty, beety, and flavorful, this sustaining soup is delightful served with the bittersweet Valentine Slaw (p. 296) and a bowl of Quinoa Pilaf (p. 290—quinoa is another heart-healthy food).

Procedure

1. Heat the oil in a 3-quart pot over high heat. Add the leek and garlic and sauté for a few minutes until they begin to brown.

2. Add the remaining ingredients except the spinach or chard and bring to a boil. Reduce the heat to medium, cover, and simmer for 15 minutes or until the beet is tender.

3. Add the spinach or chard and let it wilt for a couple of minutes. Remove from the heat, ladle into bowls, and serve.

Hands-on prep time: 15 minutes
Cook time: 25 minutes
Total time: 35 minutes
Makes about 6 cups

Ingredients

1 tsp oil

1 cup finely sliced leek (1-2 leeks)

1 tsp minced garlic

4 cups water

2 cups diced beet (1-2 beets)

1 cup cooked or canned kidney beans (rinsed and drained)

⅔ cup diced tomato

1 tsp minced ginger

1 tsp minced fresh rosemary

1 tsp salt or ¼ cup Bragg Liquid Aminos or to taste

¼ cup pitted, chopped kalamata olives (about 10 olives)

2 cups chopped spinach or chard

Potato Chard Chowder

Relax & Restore

Soothing and strengthening, this restorative recipe is quick and easy to make. Herbs like basil and rosemary promote a clear, calm mind. Miso and mineral-rich potato (the ultimate comfort food) help alleviate acid conditions in the body, while emerald-colored chard provides a wealth of calcium, magnesium, and chlorophyll, helping to nourish hungry cells and soothe frayed nerves.

Procedure

1. Place the water, salt, potato, and beans in a 3-quart pot and bring to a boil over high heat. Reduce the heat to medium, cover, and simmer for about 10 minutes or until the potato is tender.

2. Meanwhile, place the pumpkin seeds in a small skillet over medium heat and toast for a few minutes, stirring occasionally, until they begin to puff up and brown. Add the Braggs or tamari and stir for a few seconds until dry. Remove from the heat and transfer to a bowl.

3. When the potato is just tender, add the zucchini and chard to the soup and simmer for another 5 minutes or until the chard is completely wilted. Remove from the heat.

4. Ladle ⅓ cup of the broth into a cup and combine with the miso until smooth. Add this mixture to the soup along with the vinegar, basil, and rosemary. Ladle into bowls, garnish with the pumpkin seeds, and serve.

Tips/Variations

Serve with side bowls of brown rice sprinkled with gomasio.

> **Hands-on prep time:** 15 minutes
> **Cook time:** 20 minutes
> **Total time:** 20 minutes
> **Makes** about 6 cups

Ingredients

- 3½ cups water
- ½ tsp salt or to taste
- 2 cups chopped potato (1-2 potatoes)
- ½ cup frozen shelled soybeans (edamame) or baby lima beans
- 2 Tbsp raw pumpkin seeds for garnishing
- ½ tsp Bragg Liquid Aminos or tamari
- 1 cup chopped zucchini
- 2 cups finely chopped chard (2-3 large leaves)
- 3 Tbsp white or yellow miso
- 1-2 Tbsp apple cider vinegar
- 1 Tbsp minced fresh basil
- 1 tsp minced fresh rosemary

Wasabi Noodle Soup

Slim & Trim

The energizing influences of wasabi, ginger, shiitake, daikon radish, chili, sesame oil, and watercress help boost a sluggish metabolism, while the cleansing diuretic properties of bean sprouts and nori help relieve water retention. Serve this soup as a light lunch or supper with the zesty Daikon Slaw (p. 297).

Procedure

1. Prepare the noodles according to the package directions, rinse under cold water, and strain. With a pair of scissors, cut noodles into bite-size lengths (about 2-3 inches long). Set aside.

2. Place the water, tofu, Braggs or tamari, ginger, and wasabi in a blender and blend until smooth. Pour the mixture into a 2-quart pot and place over medium-low heat.

3. Meanwhile, heat the oil in a small skillet over medium-high heat. Add the mushrooms, garlic, and salt and sauté for a few minutes until the mushrooms are nicely browned. Remove from the heat and set aside.

4. Add the noodles, sautéed mushrooms, sprouts, and watercress to the soup, increase the heat to medium-high, and bring the soup to just under a boil (do not boil or the tofu will curdle). Add a little more water if necessary and Braggs or tamari to taste. Remove from the heat. Ladle into bowls, garnish with nori, green onion, and chili (optional), and serve immediately with slices of lime.

Hands-on prep time: 15 minutes
Cook time: 15 minutes
Total time: 25 minutes
Makes about 4 cups

Ingredients

1 small bundle dried bean thread noodles (a.k.a. glass or mung noodles, 1.5 ounces)

4 cups water

6 ounces firm silken tofu

¼ cup Bragg Liquid Aminos or tamari or to taste

1 Tbsp minced ginger

1 tsp wasabi powder or paste

1 tsp toasted sesame oil

1 cup sliced shiitake mushrooms (stems removed)

1 tsp minced garlic

Dash of salt

½ cup chopped bean sprouts

1 cup chopped watercress (or more if desired)

Garnishes

1 sheet nori seaweed, finely slivered (use scissors)

1 Tbsp minced green onion

½ tsp minced fresh chili or red chili flakes (optional)

Lime slices

Fat Burner

Slim & Trim

Here's an easy, beautifully flavored soup that my body just craves. Small, soft, and very easy to digest, adzukis are one of the most pleasant members of the bean family. Together with jerusalem artichoke, seaweed, celery, arugula, and cucumber, they make an excellent soup to promote weight loss, kidney vitality, and detoxification. This recipe also helps reduce fluid retention. It's delicious served with the spicy Slimming Slaw (p. 296).

Plan ahead: For quicker cooking, maximum nutrition, and easy digestion, soak the adzuki beans at room temperature for about 6 hours first. They will expand to more than 1 cup, but still use all of them.

Procedure

1. Place all the ingredients except the arugula and cucumber in a 4-quart pot and bring to a boil over high heat. Reduce the heat to medium, cover, and simmer for 20 minutes or until the adzuki beans are tender.

2. Remove from the heat, ladle into bowls and garnish with arugula and cucumber (optional).

> Soak time: About 6 hours
> Hands-on prep time: 20 minutes
> Cook time: 30 minutes
> Total time: 40 minutes (not including soak time)
> Makes about 9 cups

Ingredients

8 cups water

1 cup dried adzuki beans
(soaked and drained)

2 cups peeled, chopped jerusalem artichoke

1 cup chopped celery (2 stalks)

1 cup finely sliced leek (1-2 leeks)

2 Tbsp minced ginger

2 tsp crumbled hijiki or arame seaweed

½ tsp dry mustard

1 tsp ground coriander

¼ tsp turmeric

Cayenne pepper to taste

⅓ cup Bragg Liquid Aminos or tamari or to taste

2 cups chopped arugula
for garnishing

¼ cup julienned cucumber
for garnishing (optional)

Raw Energizer

According to Ayurveda, almonds are one of the most thoroughly nourishing foods for our bodies, providing subtle components we need for growth and vitality. Light, creamy, and completely raw, here they make an energizing soup that's an absolute breeze to prepare. Living sprouts are also nutritional powerhouses—full of minerals, vitamins, protein, enzymes, and antioxidants. With apple cider vinegar and cayenne, this recipe makes a wonderful summertime pick-me-up.

Plan ahead: Soak the almonds in 4 cups of water for 8 to 12 hours at room temperature to let them germinate. This enlivens the almonds, making them more nutritious (and less fattening).

Procedure

1. Strain the almonds and rinse. Place the almonds, water, Braggs or tamari, vinegar, green onion, and ginger in a blender and blend until smooth. Pour into large bowl, add the salad veggies, and chill for 1 hour. Meanwhile, combine the mango and mint in a small bowl.

2. Pour the soup into bowls, garnish with the minted mango, sprouts, and cayenne, and serve.

Tips/Variations

Serve with cucumber sushi rolls or roasted veggie wraps.

Soak time: 8-12 hours
Hands-on prep time: 10 minutes
Chill time: 1 hour
Total time: 1 hour 10 minutes (not including soak time)
Makes about 5 cups

Ingredients

- 1½ cups raw almonds, soaked*
- 3 cups water
- ¼ cup Bragg Liquid Aminos or tamari or to taste
- 1 Tbsp apple cider vinegar
- 2 green onions, bases and tops trimmed
- 1-inch piece ginger, peeled
- 1 cup diced crunchy salad veggies (like cucumber, bell pepper, or jicama)
- 1 cup diced mango (1 large mango) for garnishing
- 2 Tbsp minced fresh mint leaves plus whole leaves for garnishing
- 1 cup pea shoots or sunflower sprouts for garnishing
- Cayenne pepper to taste for garnishing

*The almonds will expand to just over 2 cups after soaking. Use all of them.

Everfresh Soup

Strength & Energy

This refreshing and sophisticated soup is sweet, light, and subtly energizing. It makes the perfect appetizer to a healthy summer meal. Nourishing corn and protein-packed sunflower sprouts help replenish chi, making this recipe an excellent energy tonic that promotes a feeling of lightness in the body.

Plan ahead: If using fresh corn on the cob, you'll need to cook it first. This takes an additional 15 minutes.

Procedure

1. Place the water and corn in a blender and blend until smooth. Strain through a fine sieve or through 2 layers of cheesecloth into a 2-quart pot.

2. Add the carrot, snow peas, bell pepper, and Cajun seasoning and gently bring to just under a boil over medium-high heat.

3. Remove from the heat and stir in the lime juice, cilantro, and salt to taste. Serve warm, or chill for 1½ hours and serve garnished with sprouts (optional).

Tips/Variations

Mango variation: Add ½ cup diced mango along with the lime juice and cilantro.

Serve with wholegrain rolls and a zesty mesclun salad.

> **Hands-on prep time:** 20 minutes
> **Cook time:** 10 minutes
> **Chill time:** 1 hour 30 minutes (optional)
> **Total time:** 30 minutes (or more with chilling)
> **Makes** about 5 cups

Ingredients

- **3 cups water**
- **5 cups cooked fresh corn kernels*** (cut from 7-8 large ears, or use frozen corn, thawed)
- **½ cup thinly sliced carrot**
- **8 snow peas, strings removed and finely sliced**
- **2 Tbsp diced red bell pepper**
- **1 tsp Cajun seasoning or to taste**
- **2 Tbsp lime juice**
- **3 Tbsp minced cilantro**
- **Salt to taste**
- **½ cup sunflower sprouts** for garnishing if serving chilled (optional)

*Bring a few inches of water to a boil over high heat in a large stock pot. Meanwhile, husk the corn. When water is boiling, add the corn and cover with a tight-fitting lid. Cook for 5 minutes, then remove from heat. Fill pot with cold water to cool the corn.

Almond Broccoli Soup

Strong Bones

Rich in calcium, magnesium, and protein, almonds help strengthen and renew bone and tissues while alkalizing the body and supporting the lungs. Add a cup of calcium-rich tofu and this recipe is even more beneficial to your bones—as well as a complete meal.

Plan ahead: Soak the almonds in 3 cups of water for 8 to 12 hours at room temperature to let them germinate. This enlivens the almonds, making them more nutritious (and less fattening).

Procedure

1. Strain the almonds and rinse. Place the soaked almonds and water in a blender and blend until smooth. Strain the pulp through a fine sieve, pressing the pulp with the back of a spoon to release the milk. (Alternatively, you can strain through a colander lined with 2 layers of cheesecloth, then twist the cloth to squeeze out all the milk.) Discard the pulp.

2. Place the almond milk in a 3-quart pot over medium-high heat. Add the broccoli, bok choy, tarragon, sage, and pepper. Bring to just under a boil, reduce the heat to medium-low, and simmer for 5 to 7 minutes until the broccoli is tender.

3. Meanwhile, heat the oil in a small skillet over high heat. Add the mushrooms, garlic, and salt and sauté for a few minutes until they begin to brown. Add this to the soup.

4. Remove the soup from the heat. Add the Braggs or ladle ½ cup of broth into a cup and combine with the miso until smooth; stir this into the soup. Ladle into bowls and serve.

> **Soak time:** 8-12 hours
> **Hands-on prep time:** 15 minutes
> **Cook time:** 20 minutes
> **Total time:** 30 minutes (not including soak time)
> **Makes** about 6 cups

Ingredients

1 cup raw almonds, soaked*
4 cups water
2 cups bite-size broccoli florets
1 cup shredded bok choy
1 tsp minced fresh tarragon
½ tsp dried rubbed sage
¼ tsp black pepper
1 tsp oil
1 cup sliced cremini or button mushrooms
1½ tsp fresh minced garlic (1-2 cloves)
¼ tsp salt
¼ cup Bragg Liquid Aminos or white or yellow miso

*The almonds will expand to about 1½ cups after soaking. Use all of them.

Stews

Curl up by a roaring fire with a comfy
blanket and a hearty bowl of stew.

Hearty Chili

Here's a delicious stew that's long been in demand by my son and his friends. Instead of corn, I usually use hominy, which can be fried beforehand if you prefer. Like most good chili, this one tastes even better the next day, so go ahead and double the recipe.

Procedure

1. Place the chili and water in a 1-quart pot over high heat and bring to a boil. Remove from the heat and let sit for 5 minutes until the chili softens. Place the chili and water in a blender, blend until smooth, and set aside.

2. Heat the oil in a 5-quart pot over medium-high heat. Add the onions and sauté for a few minutes until they begin to brown. Then add the garlic, bell pepper, veggie ground, and hominy or corn and sauté another 5 minutes, stirring occasionally.

3. Add the blended chili water, tomato, beans, chili powder, salt, sugar, and cocoa powder, increase the heat to high, and bring to a boil. Reduce the heat to medium-low, cover, and simmer for up to an hour, stirring occasionally. Remove from the heat, ladle into bowls, garnish with cilantro (optional), and serve.

Tips/Variations

Serve with Chili Lime Tortilla Crisps (p. 289) and grated sharp cheddar.

Hands-on prep time: 20 minutes
Cook time: 1 hour 20 minutes (maximum)
Total time: 1 hour 30 minutes (maximum)
Makes about 8 cups

Ingredients

- 1 dried roasted pasilla or chipotle chili*
- 1 cup water
- 2 Tbsp oil
- 1 cup peeled, trimmed pearl onions** or chopped onion
- 2 Tbsp minced garlic (4-6 cloves)
- 2 cups chopped green bell pepper (2 peppers)
- One 12-ounce package Yves Good Ground Veggie Original (or other vegetarian ground "beef")
- 1½ cups hominy or corn
- One 28-ounce can diced tomato (or 3½ cups fresh)
- 2 cups cooked or canned pinto or black beans (rinsed and drained)
- 1 tsp chili powder
- 2 tsp salt or to taste
- 1½ tsp brown sugar
- 1 tsp unsweetened cocoa powder (or ½ square baking chocolate)
- ½ cup minced cilantro for garnishing (optional)

*You can find dried chilies in the produce section of many grocery stores. If you can't find any, use 1 or 2 canned chipotles instead. No need to boil, simply blend.

**You can easily remove the pearl onion skins by blanching them first (see p. 16).

Gumbo

There are thousands of ways to prepare this Cajun classic, but I like this healthy, hearty veggie version. It uses flavorful vegetarian meat substitutes, which are available in most grocery stores. Feel free to experiment with your favorites.

Procedure

1. Heat 1½ tablespoons of the oil in a 5-quart pot over high heat. Add the onion, celery, and garlic and sauté for a few minutes until they begin to brown.

2. Add the flour to the pot and mix well, allowing it to brown slightly for a minute or two. Gradually stir in the water, then add the tomato sauce, okra, root beer (optional), worcestershire sauce, Cajun seasoning, bay leaves, sage, pepper, and bouillon cubes. Bring to a boil, reduce the heat to medium, cover, and simmer for 10 minutes.

3. Meanwhile, heat the remaining 1½ tablespoons oil in a large skillet. Add the veggie chicken and sausage and pan-fry for 5 to 10 minutes, stirring occasionally, until golden brown and crispy. Add them to the stew.

4. Remove the stew from the heat, stir in the parsley (optional), and salt to taste if necessary. Ladle into bowls and serve.

Tips/Variations

For a "fishy" gumbo: Add 1 to 2 tablespoons crumbled hijiki or arame seaweed in Step 3 and swap the vegetarian sausage for vegetarian salmon (or use both).

Hands-on prep time: 15 minutes
Cook time: 25 minutes
Total time: 35 minutes
Makes about 10 cups

Ingredients

3 Tbsp oil

¾ cup chopped onion

¾ cup chopped celery (2 stalks)

1½ Tbsp minced garlic (3-5 cloves)

½ cup unbleached white flour

6 cups water

1¼ cups tomato sauce

1½ cups sliced okra (rounds)

⅓ cup root beer (optional)

1-2 Tbsp vegetarian worcestershire sauce

2-3 tsp Cajun seasoning

3 bay leaves

1 tsp dried rubbed sage

1 tsp black pepper

2 veggie bouillon cubes (chicken-style)

One 8-ounce package vegetarian chicken burgers, cubed (2 cups)

One 8-ounce package vegetarian sausage, chopped (2 cups)

¼ cup minced parsley (optional)

Salt to taste

Homestyle Seitan Stew

Whether your in-laws are coming for dinner or your son and his friends have just arrived, this simple, substantial stew makes everyone feel right at home. Rich with meaty mushrooms and succulent seitan, it's a well-used recipe that inspires kids to eat their vegetables—and enjoy them.

Procedure

1. Heat the oil in a 5-quart pot over high heat. Add the onion, bell pepper, celery, mushrooms, garlic, seitan, and ¼ teaspoon of the salt and sauté for a few minutes until the vegetables begin to soften.

2. Add the remaining ingredients (including the remaining 1½ teaspoons of salt) and bring to a boil. Reduce the heat to medium, cover, and simmer for about 20 minutes or longer if desired. Remove from the heat and serve.

Tips/Variations

Serve with warm garlic bread and a simple green salad with toasted hazelnuts.

Hands-on prep time: 15 minutes
Cook time: 30 minutes
Total time: 45 minutes
Makes about 10 cups

Ingredients

2 Tbsp oil

1 cup chopped onion

2 cups chopped green bell pepper (2 peppers)

1 cup chopped celery (2 stalks)

2 cups sliced cremini or button mushrooms

3 Tbsp minced garlic (6-8 cloves)

One 8-ounce package unseasoned seitan, chopped (bite-size, about 2 cups)

1¾ tsp salt or to taste

One 15-ounce can diced tomato (or 2 cups fresh)

2 cups water

2 cups cubed potato (2 potatoes)

1½ cups cubed turnip

1½ cups chopped carrot (2-3 carrots)

3 bay leaves

2 tsp Italian seasoning

¼ tsp whole black peppercorns

Hungarian Goulash

Perfect for everyday family fare, tasty goulash is also great to bring along to potlucks and holiday dinners. Seasoned TVP Nuggets make it hearty and appealing to vegetarians and non-vegetarians alike.

Procedure

1. Heat the oil in a 5-quart pot over high heat. Add the onion and sauté for a minute until it begins to brown. Add the garlic and caraway seeds and sauté for another minute.

2. Add the water, potato, carrot, rutabaga or turnip, paprika, and Spike. Bring to a boil, reduce the heat to medium, cover, and simmer for 15 to 20 minutes. Meanwhile, prepare the TVP.

3. Add the cabbage and cook for another 10 minutes. Then add the TVP nuggets and salt and pepper to taste. Remove from the heat, ladle into bowls, and serve.

Tips/Variations

TVP variation: You can use seitan or tofu in place of the TVP. No need to boil first; simply pan-fry with the seasonings (see p. 293).

Serve with fluffy warm bread for dipping or over steamed brown rice. Goulash is also wonderful with pierogies and sour cream.

> Hands-on prep time: 15 minutes
> Cook time: 40 minutes
> Total time: 50 minutes
> Makes about 10 cups

Ingredients

1 Tbsp oil

1 cup chopped onion

1 Tbsp minced garlic (2-3 cloves)

½ tsp caraway seeds

8 cups water

3 cups chopped potato (3 potatoes)

1 cup chopped carrot (1-2 carrots)

2 cups diced rutabaga or turnip

2 tsp paprika

3½ Tbsp Spike

1 recipe Seasoned TVP Nuggets (p. 293)

2 cups chopped cabbage

Salt and pepper to taste

Seitan Stroganoff

Everyone will love coming home to a warm, nourishing bowl of stroganoff. With hearty seitan, yucca, mushrooms, pasta, and cashews, it's a robustly flavored everyman's stew. You needn't serve it with anything but fluffy slices of bread to soak up the luscious broth.

Procedure

1. Place 8 cups of the water, 1 teaspoon of the salt, and the yucca in a 4-quart pot and bring to a boil over high heat. Add the fettuccine, reduce the heat to medium-high, and cook for 10 to 12 minutes, stirring occasionally, until both are just tender. Strain and rinse well with cold water, gently separating the noodles with a fork if necessary. Set aside.

2. Meanwhile, heat the oil in a 6-quart pot over high heat. Add the onion, celery, garlic, mushrooms, seitan, and ½ teaspoon of the salt and sauté for a few minutes until the mushrooms begin to brown. Add the sherry and cook for another 2 minutes.

3. Add 4½ cups of the water, the remaining 2½ teaspoons salt, and the tomato, sour cream, pepper, thyme, and cashews, as well as the cooked yucca and fettuccine. Bring to a boil, stirring occasionally.

4. Meanwhile, combine the remaining ½ cup water with the flour until they form a smooth paste. Add this paste to the stew, stirring constantly so no lumps form. Cook for a few minutes, then remove from the heat, ladle into bowls, and serve.

Tips/Variations

Yucca alternative: If you don't have yucca on hand, use potato instead.

Garnish possibilities: Fresh-grated parmesan, fresh-ground pepper, and/or minced Italian parsley.

Hands-on prep time:	20 minutes
Cook time:	25 minutes
Total time:	35 minutes
Makes	about 12 cups

Ingredients

13 cups water

4 tsp salt or to taste

2 cups peeled, chopped yucca

6 ounces fettuccine, broken into 2-inch segments

2 Tbsp oil

1 cup chopped onion

1 cup chopped celery (2 stalks)

1 Tbsp minced garlic (2-3 cloves)

1½ cups sliced button or cremini mushrooms (6 ounces)

One 8-ounce package unseasoned seitan, chopped (bite-size, about 2 cups)

½ cup sherry

One 15-ounce can diced tomato

1 cup sour cream

1 tsp black pepper

2 tsp dried thyme

¾ cup unsalted roasted cashews

¼ cup unbleached white flour

Ratatouille

Ratatouille is one recipe that makes me truly appreciate my garden. It's a casual one-pot wonder that's perfect for celebrating flavorful vegetables. With couscous, quinoa, or roasted potatoes, it's easily the centerpiece of a meal. It can also be part of a Mediterranean grazing spread alongside tabouleh, pita bread, and falafels. Serve Ratatouille warm, chilled, or at room temperature.

Procedure

1. Heat the oil in a 5-quart pot over high heat. Add the onion and garlic and sauté for a few minutes until they begin to brown. Add the remaining ingredients except the pine nuts (toss the veggies into the pot as you chop them). Bring to a boil, reduce the heat to medium, cover, and simmer for about 20 minutes or until the eggplant is tender, stirring occasionally.

2. Stir in the pine nuts and remove from the heat. Ladle into bowls, garnish with sprigs of fresh rosemary, and serve.

Tips/Variations

Optional additions: Add ½ teaspoon minced fresh chili or red chili flakes as well as 3 tablespoons capers and/or slivered sun-dried tomatoes.

> Hands-on prep time: 20 minutes
> Cook time: 35 minutes
> Total time: 45 minutes
> Makes about 9 cups

Ingredients

2 Tbsp oil

1½ cups roughly chopped red onion

2 Tbsp minced garlic
(4-6 cloves)

5 cups cubed eggplant*
(1 large eggplant)

1½ cups roughly chopped red bell pepper (1-2 peppers)

1 cup roughly chopped carrot
(1-2 carrots)

4½ cups chopped tomato
(5-7 tomatoes or two 19-ounce cans)

2 Tbsp balsamic vinegar

2 tsp salt

1 tsp sugar

1 tsp minced fresh rosemary
plus whole sprigs for garnishing

1 Tbsp fresh thyme leaves
(or 1 tsp dried)

1 tsp dried oregano

¼ cup chopped pitted olives
(I recommend kalamata)

2 cups chopped zucchini*
(1-2 zucchini)

¼ cup toasted pine nuts**

*You may wish to salt the eggplant before tossing it in the pot, and possibly the zucchini too (see p. 13 for method). Test them first to see if they're bitter.

**See Toasting Nuts and Seeds, p. 10.

Chilled

Chilled soups are great in the summer because they let you enjoy a light, healthy soup without breaking a sweat. Note that if you use primarily chilled ingredients, you'll eliminate most chill times.

Arugula Vichyssoise

I love vichyssoise because it's rich and creamy, yet at the same time refreshing and delicate. In this simple recipe, I use arugula instead of leek, which keeps it light and peppery. Serve chilled or at room temperature.

Plan ahead: If you think of it, cook the potatoes and refrigerate them the night before. This will eliminate the chill time.

Procedure

1. Steam the potato for about 20 minutes or until tender.

2. Heat the butter in a small skillet over medium-high heat. Add the onion and garlic and sauté for a few minutes until golden brown.

3. Place 3 cups of the steamed potato, the water, and the sautéed onion and garlic in a blender and blend until smooth. Transfer to a 3-quart bowl and add the remaining 3 cups steamed potato and the cream, arugula, and salt and combine thoroughly. Chill for at least an hour.

4. Ladle into bowls, garnish with arugula and pepper, and serve.

Hands-on prep time: 15 minutes
Cook time: 20 minutes
Chill time: 1-2 hours
Total time: 30 minutes (not including chill time)
Makes about 8 cups

Ingredients

6 cups cubed, unpeeled red potato (5-6 potatoes)

2 Tbsp butter

1 cup chopped onion

1 Tbsp minced garlic (2-3 cloves)

3 cups cold water

1⅓ cups heavy whipping cream

1½ cups chopped arugula plus extra for garnishing

2 tsp salt or to taste

Fresh-ground black pepper to taste for garnishing

Greek Goddess

This healthy, protein-packed Mediterranean soup gets its rich creaminess and distinct flavor from blended chickpeas, calcium-rich tahini, and jerusalem artichoke. It's excellent for anyone minding their blood sugar.

Procedure

1. Place the jerusalem artichoke and 2 cups of the water in a small pot over high heat, cover, and bring to a boil. Reduce the heat to medium and simmer for 15 minutes or until the artichoke is tender. Remove from the heat, strain, and set aside to cool.

2. Meanwhile, heat the oil in a small skillet over high heat. Add the onion and garlic and sauté for a few minutes until they begin to brown. Remove from the heat.

3. In batches, place half the artichoke, the sautéed onion and garlic, and the remaining 3 cups of water as well as the tahini, lemon juice, salt, basil, parsley, and 1½ cups of the chickpeas in a blender and blend until smooth.

4. Transfer to a 3-quart bowl, add the remaining artichoke and remaining 1 cup of chickpeas, and chill for 1½ to 2 hours or until ready to serve.

5. Ladle into bowls, garnish with the olives, paprika, and sprouts (optional), and serve.

Tips/Variations

Veggie add-ins: This soup is also delicious with a cup of steamed broccoli florets, baby green beans, or spinach.

Have it hot: You can serve it warm too, but don't bring it to a boil as the tahini will curdle slightly. When serving it hot, skip the sunflower sprout garnish.

> Hands-on prep time: 20 minutes
> Cook time: 20 minutes
> Chill time: 1½-2 hours
> Total time: 30 minutes (not including chill time)
> Makes about 7 cups

Ingredients

- 3 cups peeled, cubed jerusalem artichoke
- 5 cups water
- 1 Tbsp oil
- ½ cup chopped onion
- 1 Tbsp minced garlic (2-3 cloves)
- ¼ cup tahini
- 3 Tbsp lemon juice
- 2 tsp salt or to taste
- ½ cup fresh basil (packed)
- ½ cup fresh parsley (packed)
- 2½ cups cooked or canned chickpeas (rinsed and drained)
- 2 Tbsp sliced pitted green olives (regular or pimiento) for garnishing
- Paprika for garnishing
- 1 cup sunflower sprouts for garnishing (optional)

Cocktail Tomato Soup

The first time I made this recipe was for a Sunday brunch, and it certainly made a good substitute for coffee! Spicy and flavorful, this is a fun soup that's great for summer entertaining because there are lots of clever ways to present it. You can serve it in a glass pitcher and then pour it into stemmed glasses rimmed with celery salt. Colorful bowls, mugs, or teacups are also cute.

Procedure

1. In batches, place the vegetable juice, roasted bell peppers, and parsley in a blender and blend until smooth.

2. Pour the mixture into a 4-quart bowl or pitcher, add the remaining ingredients except the garnishes, and combine well. Chill for an hour if desired (unnecessary if ingredients are already chilled).

3. Meanwhile, prepare the celery garnish. To do so, place the cream cheese, horseradish, and honey in a 1-quart bowl and mash with a fork until smooth and well combined. Use a butter knife or icing bag (with a large star tip) to fill each celery stalk.

4. Ladle or pour the soup into bowls, glasses, or mugs and serve each with a celery stalk and a slice of lime or lemon.

Tips/Variations

Fresh veggie juice variation: Instead of store-bought vegetable juice, you can use 5 cups fresh tomato blended with 1 to 2 cups water until very smooth. Add salt to taste, starting with 1 teaspoon.

> **Hands-on prep time:** 20 minutes
> **Chill time:** 1 hour (if necessary)
> **Total time:** 20 minutes (not including chill time)
> **Makes** about 9 cups

Ingredients

6 cups V8 vegetable juice (or other favorite)

1 cup roasted red bell peppers*

½ cup roughly chopped Italian parsley (loosely packed)

1 cup finely diced tomato (1-2 tomatoes)

1 cup finely chopped celery heart (pale inner stalks)

Tabasco or other hot sauce to taste

2 Tbsp lime or lemon juice

1-2 Tbsp prepared horseradish

2 tsp vegetarian worcestershire sauce (optional)

1 tsp onion powder

½ tsp celery salt

Fresh-ground black pepper to taste

Lime or lemon slices for garnishing

Celery Garnish

1 8-ounce package cream cheese (room temperature)

4 Tbsp prepared horseradish

2 tsp honey

6-9 whole celery stalks

*If using store-bought roasted peppers, gently rinse and drain them first. If roasting them yourself, see p. 12 for an easy method.

Cucumber Raita Soup

with Pineapple Chutney and Curry Potatoes

Raita is a salad-like side dish that's traditional in Indian cuisine. It's simple, cooling, helpful to digestion, and brings a light, fresh touch to any meal. It's no wonder my friend Nadia was inspired to create a soup in its honor. During summer, she serves Cucumber Raita Soup as an appetizer to a feast of chickpea curry, spicy vegetable samosas, basmati rice, and crispy papadams.

Plan ahead: This soup works best when the cucumber and onion soften up first. To achieve this effect—as well as a fuller flavor—try preparing this soup in the morning, then chill until lunch or suppertime. Remember that the potatoes need time to cool to room temperature, so make them a good hour before serving.

Procedure

1. Combine all the soup ingredients in a 3-quart bowl and chill until the cucumber and onion have softened slightly. Meanwhile, prepare the potatoes and then the chutney (see next page).

2. Ladle the soup into bowls and garnish with the potatoes and then the chutney.

Hands-on prep time: 30 minutes
Cook time: 20 minutes
Chill time: Minimum 1 hour
Total time: 1 hour 40 minutes
Makes about 6 cups soup plus add-ins (4 good servings)

Ingredients

2 cups low-fat yogurt

1 cup low-fat buttermilk

1 cup water

2 cups peeled, julienned seedless cucumber

2 Tbsp finely slivered red onion

1 tsp minced garlic

¼ cup minced cilantro or mint leaves

½ tsp salt

1 recipe Curry Potatoes (p. 246)

1 recipe Pineapple Chutney (p. 246)

Enliven a Recipe with Chutney

An ancient culinary tradition from India, chutneys are the perfect way to enliven a soup or any other type of recipe. They lend diversity to each bite and they can enhance digestion and nutrition as well. The word "chutney" comes from the East Indian term *chatni*, which means "strongly spiced." Though there are thousands of chutney formulas, ranging from mild and sweet to hot and pungent, these tasty condiments typically have intense, distinct flavors. Just a spoonful can take a recipe to another dimension.

Curry Potatoes

Ingredients

1½ Tbsp ghee or oil
½ tsp cumin seeds
½ tsp black mustard seeds
1½ cups finely cubed yukon gold potato (¼-inch cubes, 1-2 potatoes)
¼ tsp turmeric
⅓ cup water
¼ tsp salt

Procedure

Heat the ghee or oil in a medium skillet over high heat. Add the cumin and mustard seeds and cook for a few seconds, then add the potato. Pan-fry over high heat until the potato begins to turn golden brown. Add the turmeric, water, and salt and reduce the heat to medium. Cover and simmer until there is no more water and the potato is tender, about 10 to 15 minutes. Add a little more water if you need to. Remove from the heat and cool until room temperature (about an hour).

Pineapple Chutney

Ingredients

1½ cups chopped pineapple (if canned, drained)
⅓ cup minced cilantro
¾ tsp minced ginger
2 Tbsp sugar
½ tsp cinnamon
½ tsp ground coriander
¼ tsp nutmeg
¼ tsp allspice
⅛ tsp turmeric
½ tsp minced fresh chili or red chili flakes

Procedure

Combine all the ingredients in a 1-quart bowl and chill until needed.

Minted Pea Bisque

Energizing and low in fat, this simple soup is a welcome refreshment on a hot summer day. As a light lunch, brunch, or appetizer, it's lovely served with chilled summer rolls, a cool Asian noodle dish, or a light grain salad like tabouleh. Mint and ginger are gentle stimulants that give this soup an invigorating, uplifting quality.

Procedure

In batches, place all the ingredients except the sugar snap peas in a blender and blend until smooth. Transfer to a 3-quart bowl. Add the sugar snap peas, mix, and chill for an hour if desired (unnecessary if ingredients are already chilled). Stir well, ladle into bowls, garnish with mint, and serve.

Tips/Variations

For a creamier soup: Blend with 1 cup avocado or coconut milk.

Hands-on prep time: 10 minutes
Chill time: 1 hour (if necessary)
Total time: 10 minutes (not including chill time)
Makes about 8 cups

Ingredients

4 cups cold water

6 cups fresh or frozen (thawed) peas

⅓ cup unsweetened desiccated coconut

⅓ cup honey

3 cups mint leaves (gently packed) plus extra for garnishing

¼ cup chopped ginger

¼ cup lime juice

1 tsp salt or to taste

2 dozen sugar snap peas, sliced

Chilled Cauliflower Curry

Bursting with beautiful flavors, this sumptuous coconut curry makes an elegant summer appetizer or light meal. I find it tastes best at room temperature.

Plan ahead: This recipe calls for Vegetarian Chicken Broth (p. 283). It also requires a total of 9 cups cauliflower, which is equivalent to two medium heads.

Procedure

1. Preheat the oven to 400°F.

2. Spread 3 cups of the cauliflower florets in a metal roasting pan, spray with oil, and sprinkle with ¼ teaspoon of the salt. Bake for 30 minutes or until golden, tender, and slightly shriveled.

3. Meanwhile, steam the yam for 10 minutes. Add the remaining 6 cups cauliflower and steam for another 10 minutes or until both the yam and cauliflower are tender. Remove from the heat.

4. In batches, place the steamed yam and cauliflower, coconut milk, water or broth, bouillon cube (if using water), and remaining 1 teaspoon salt in a blender and blend until smooth. Transfer to a 5-quart pot.

5. Heat the ghee, butter, or oil in a small skillet over medium-high heat. Add the onion and sauté for a few minutes until it begins to brown. Add the coriander, cumin, mustard, and fennel seeds and sauté for a minute until the seeds darken and begin to pop. Add the curry powder and sauté for another few seconds. Remove from the heat.

6. Add the sautéed spices, roasted cauliflower, and peas to the pot and stir through. Cool to room temperature and serve (or serve warm if you can't wait).

> **Hands-on prep time:** 15 minutes
> **Cook time:** 35 minutes (not including Vegetarian Chicken Broth time)
> **Chill time:** 1-2 hours
> **Total time:** 45 minutes
> **Makes** about 12 cups

Ingredients

9 cups bite-size cauliflower florets

Oil spray

1¼ tsp salt or to taste

4 cups cubed yam (2 yams)

One 14-ounce can coconut milk

5 cups Vegetarian Chicken Broth (p. 283)

1 veggie bouillon cube (if using water)

2 Tbsp ghee, butter, or oil

1 cup chopped onion

1 tsp coriander seeds

1 tsp cumin seeds

1 tsp black mustard seeds

1 tsp fennel seeds

1 Tbsp madras curry powder

½ cup frozen peas

Avocado Lime Soup

The first time she tried this, my friend Allison said, "I could eat 6 bowls!" Fortunately, there wasn't enough soup for that, but there was definitely enough for seconds. With a silken texture and subtle citrus zing, this festive-looking soup is truly a knockout. Good-quality avocados make a world of difference. If yours are unripe, overripe, or simply not that good, I'd make a different soup.

Procedure

1. In batches, place the avocado, water, lime juice, tomato, cilantro, celery, salt, chili, and lime leaves in a blender and blend until smooth.

2. Pour into a 3-quart bowl and stir in the corn and jicama or cucumber. Chill for up to 2 hours if necessary. Meanwhile, make croutons. Ladle soup into bowls, garnish with cilantro, bell pepper, and croutons, and serve.

> **Hands-on prep time:** 20 minutes
> **Cook time:** 15 minutes for croutons
> **Chill time:** Up to 2 hours
> **Total time:** 30 minutes (not including chill time)
> **Makes** about 8 cups

Ingredients

- **3 cups avocado** (3-4 avocados)
- **3½-4 cups water**
- **2 Tbsp lime juice**
- **1 cup chopped fresh tomato**
- **½ cup chopped cilantro** (tightly packed) plus extra for garnishing
- **¼ cup chopped celery**
- **1½ tsp salt or to taste**
- **1 small fresh chili** (stem removed) or **½ tsp red chili flakes**
- **4 small kaffir lime leaves, deveined**
- **1 cup fresh or frozen (thawed) corn**
- **½ cup peeled, diced jicama or cucumber**
- **¼ cup minced red bell pepper** for garnishing
- **1 recipe Savory Croutons** (p. 288) for garnishing

Spring Borscht

This easy sweet-yet-savory soup is a powerhouse of nutrition. While the root vegetables are grounding and nourishing, the baby vegetables and refreshing broth provide clean flavors that leave you feeling light, healthy, and energized. Lovely warm or chilled, it's perfect to make during the spring harvest.

Procedure

1. Heat the oil in a 5-quart pot over medium heat, add the fennel seeds, and sauté for a couple of minutes until they turn dark brown.

2. Add the water, beet, parsnip, carrot, fennel bulb, onions, and salt and bring to a boil over high heat. Reduce the heat to medium-low, cover, and simmer for about 10 to 15 minutes until the beet and carrot are tender. Remove from the heat and add the honey and vinegar. Chill for 2 hours or until ready to serve.

3. Ladle into bowls, garnish with sour cream and fennel greens, and serve.

Tips/Variations

Fennel variation: If you're not a big fennel fan, replace the bulb with chopped celery, baby green beans, or quartered new potatoes. Use minced fresh dill, Italian parsley, or chives in place of the fennel greens. Omit the fennel seeds or use celery seeds instead.

> **Hands-on prep time:** 20 minutes
> **Cook time:** 20 minutes
> **Chill time:** 2 hours
> **Total time:** 40 minutes (not including chill time)
> **Makes** about 8 cups

Ingredients

- ½ **Tbsp oil**
- ½ **tsp fennel seeds**
- 4 **cups water**
- 3 **cups cubed beet** (3 beets)
- 1 **cup chopped parsnip** (1-2 parsnips)
- 1 **dozen baby carrots, whole or chopped**
- 1 **cup slivered fennel bulb** plus wispy greens for garnishing
- 1 **dozen peeled, trimmed pearl onions or 1 cup chopped vidalia onion**
- 1½ **tsp salt or to taste**
- 1 **Tbsp honey**
- 1-2 **Tbsp balsamic, red wine, or champagne vinegar**
- 1 **cup sour cream or Cashew Sour Cream** (p. 298) for garnishing

Gazpacho

with Avocado Mousse

This was the first chilled soup I ever made and it's been a favorite ever since. It's easy, tasty, refreshing, and versatile—meaning that even when I vary the fresh herbs or play with the quantities, it always comes out right, just as long as I use my secret ingredient: a sweet, ripe mango. If you're not a mint enthusiast, use cilantro, or combine them if you like both.

Procedure

1. Reserve ½ cup of the mango, ¼ cup of the cucumber, ½ cup of the celery, and 2 tablespoons of the onion and set aside. Finely chop these portions (you can combine them to do this).

2. In batches, place the remaining ingredients except the radish, pistachios, and mousse in a blender and blend until quite smooth.

3. Pour the mixture into a 3-quart bowl or pitcher and stir in the reserved mango, cucumber, celery, and onion as well as the radish. Chill up to 1½ hours if necessary and prepare the mousse.

4. Ladle or pour the soup into bowls, garnish with the pistachios (optional) and mousse, and serve.

Tips/Variations

Avocado Mousse variations: Blend any leftover mint or cilantro in with the mousse. You can also use chunks of ripe avocado instead of the mousse.

Serve as a light summer brunch, lunch, or appetizer along with Pita Crisps of choice (p. 289) and sparkling water.

> **Hands-on prep time:** 30 minutes
> **Chill time:** Up to 1½ hours
> **Total time:** 30 minutes (not including chill time)
> **Makes about 6 cups**

Ingredients

- 1½ cups chopped ripe mango (1-2 large mangos)
- 1¼ cups peeled, chopped seedless cucumber
- 1 cup finely chopped celery
- ½ cup chopped vidalia or other sweet onion
- One 28-ounce can diced tomato (juice included)
- 1 cup fresh mint leaves (gently packed)
- ½ tsp ground cumin
- 1 tsp salt or to taste
- Fresh-ground black pepper to taste
- 1 Tbsp raspberry or balsamic vinegar
- ½ cup chopped red radish
- ¼ cup roughly chopped pistachios for garnishing (optional)
- 1 recipe Avocado Mousse (p. 299) for garnishing

Roasted Red Pepper Carrot Bisque

Although a sophisticated soup that's great for fine dining, this silken saffron-colored purée also goes over well with kids because the texture and flavors are so soft and pleasant. Serve it chilled in the summertime and warm in the winter. It's also delicious at room temperature.

Procedure

1. Place the carrot and water in a 4-quart pot over high heat. Cover, bring to a boil, reduce the heat to medium, and simmer for 10 minutes or until the carrots are tender. Meanwhile, soak the saffron in 2 tablespoons lukewarm water.

2. Remove from the heat and strain the carrots, reserving the water (about 4 cups). Add more water to make 6 cups.

3. In batches, place all the ingredients except the garnishes in a blender and blend until smooth. Add a little more water if it seems too thick. Transfer to a 4-quart serving bowl. Chill until just cooler than room temperature.

4. Ladle into bowls, garnish with the sun-dried tomatoes and capers (optional), and serve.

Tips/Variations

Serve with Minted Couscous (p. 291) and Mediterranean Pita Crisps (p. 289).

> Hands-on prep time: 15 minutes
> Cook time: 15 minutes
> Chill time: 1-2 hours
> Total time: 20 minutes (not including chill time)
> Makes about 9 cups

Ingredients

4 cups chopped carrot (4-8 carrots)

6-7 cups water

½ tsp saffron threads (include soaking water)

1 cup roasted unsalted cashews (whole or pieces)

¾ cup roasted red peppers*

8 sun-dried tomatoes (marinated in oil) plus 4 more, slivered, for garnishing

1 small clove garlic

2 tsp minced fresh rosemary

1½ tsp salt or to taste

2 Tbsp balsamic vinegar

1-2 Tbsp capers for garnishing (optional)

*You can use store-bought or homemade. If using store-bought, rinse and pat dry. If making your own, roast 2 medium peppers (see p. 12 for an easy method).

Caesar Soup

My kids—who have always been salad lovers—asked me to create this soup when they were young. We just called it Caesar Soup, and since then it's developed quite a following. Playful and delicious, it makes for a refreshing summer appetizer. Caesar salad fans will be in heaven.

Plan ahead: If you think of it, cook the potato and refrigerate it the night before. This will eliminate the chill time. Prepare the croutons in advance.

Procedure

1. Steam the potato for 20 minutes or until tender. Rinse under cold water for a few minutes to speed up the cooling process.

2. Place 1 cup of the potato and the water, tofu, parmesan, mayonnaise, salt, capers, garlic, lemon juice, and worcestershire sauce (optional) in a blender and blend until smooth.

3. Pour into a 3-quart bowl, add the remaining potato and the pepper to taste, and stir well. Refrigerate for 1 to 2 hours until well chilled.

4. Ladle the soup into bowls, garnish with the lettuce, croutons, capers, and parmesan (in that order), and serve.

Tips/Variations

Fakin' bacon garnish: You can also garnish with simulated bacon bits.

> Hands-on prep time: 15 minutes
> Cook time: 30 minutes
> Chill time: 1-2 hours
> Total time: 35 minutes (not including chill time)
> Makes about 8 cups

Ingredients

4 cups finely cubed red potato (about 4 potatoes)

4 cups water

18 ounces firm silken tofu

¾ cup grated parmesan cheese plus extra for garnishing

½ cup eggless mayonnaise

1½ tsp salt or to taste

2 Tbsp capers plus extra for garnishing

2 Tbsp minced garlic (4-6 cloves)

⅓ cup lemon juice

3 Tbsp vegetarian worcestershire sauce (optional)

Fresh-ground black pepper to taste

1½ cups shredded iceberg lettuce for garnishing

1 recipe Savory or Italian Croutons (p. 288) for garnishing

Desserts

Dessert lovers will find sweet-tooth satisfaction with
easy, delicious recipes the whole family will love.

Citrus Mango Bisque

This zingy, refreshing fat-free dessert soup gives you a taste of the exotic in minutes. It's the perfect follow-up to a spicy pad thai meal.

Procedure

Place the water, lemongrass, and lime leaves in a blender and blend until smooth. Add the ginger, mango, orange juice, lemon juice, and honey or sugar and blend until smooth again, in batches if necessary. Pour into bowls, garnish with zest (optional), and serve.

Tips/Variations

Yogurt garnish: Delicious with a dollop of vanilla yogurt.

> Total prep time: 10 minutes
> Makes 6 cups

Ingredients

- 1 cup water
- 3 inches lemongrass stalk*
- 2 small kaffir lime leaves, deveined**
- 1 tsp minced ginger
- 6 cups chilled chopped mango (4-6 large mangos)
- 1 cup orange juice (preferably fresh-squeezed)
- 1 Tbsp lemon juice
- 1-2 Tbsp honey or sugar or to taste
- Lemon, lime, or orange zest (strands) for garnishing (optional)

*Use the tender, milky-white inner leaves just above the base. See Preparing Lemongrass, p. 12.

**See Kaffir Lime Leaf, p. 12.

Berry Nectar

Ready in five minutes, this delicate, dreamy soup is the perfect last-minute dessert. It also makes a great brunch appetizer before waffles drenched with maple syrup. The delicious combination of buttermilk and berries promotes beautiful skin.

Procedure

Place 3 cups of the berries along with the buttermilk, sugar, vanilla, and mint in a blender and blend until smooth. Pour into dessert bowls, garnish with the remaining berries and mint leaves, and serve.

Tips/Variations

Frozen berry bliss: The frothy milkshake-like consistency of this recipe comes largely from using frozen berries. You can use fresh berries instead, but you won't get the same effect.

Total prep time: 5 minutes
Makes about 7 cups

Ingredients

4½ cups frozen mixed berries

1 quart buttermilk (cold)

½-1 cup sugar (depends on sweetness of berries)

1 tsp vanilla

½ cup fresh mint leaves plus extra for garnishing

Sweet Rice

A classic Indian recipe, Sweet Rice goes down as one of my all-time favorite desserts. My friend's daughter Sam will have it only in a drinking cup, claiming, "A spoon just slows me down." There's nothing really comparable to Sweet Rice in Western cooking, so I encourage you to try it—you won't be disappointed.

Procedure

1. Place the milk and rice in a heavy-bottomed 5-quart pot and bring to a boil over medium-high heat, stirring constantly. Once it boils, immediately reduce the heat to low and simmer for 10 to 15 minutes, stirring every couple of minutes to make sure the rice doesn't stick to the bottom.

2. When the rice is cooked and floats to the top, turn off the heat and add the sugar, cardamom (optional), vanilla, rose water, and whipping cream. Stir well, cool for a couple of hours, then chill for 12 to 24 hours.

3. Remove the cardamom pods if using, ladle into bowls or cups, garnish with pistachios (optional), and serve.

Tips/Variations

Flavor variation: Instead of cardamom and rose water, try using 1 tablespoon finely minced ginger, ½ teaspoon nutmeg, and a cinnamon stick.

> Hands-on prep time: 10 minutes
> Cook time: 30 minutes
> Chill time: 12-24 hours
> Total time: 40 minutes (not including chill time)
> Makes about 8 cups

Ingredients

- 8 cups whole milk (half gallon)
- ⅔ cup white basmati rice
- 1 cup sugar
- ½ tsp ground cardamom or 4 dented cardamom pods (optional)
- 1 tsp vanilla
- 1 tsp rose water
- 1 cup whipping cream (half pint)
- ½ cup chopped, toasted pistachios* for garnishing (optional)

*See Toasting Nuts and Seeds, p. 10.

Warm Apple Harvest

While shooting my show in New Zealand one fall, we became good friends with the neighbors, who had a small but plentiful orchard of sweet-tart macintosh apples. We came up with all kinds of neat ways to use them, including this cozy soup that everyone on the crew just loved. It tastes even better with vanilla ice cream.

Procedure

Crumble Topping

1. Preheat the oven to 325°F.

2. Place the butter, sugar, and vanilla in a 3-quart bowl and combine well. Add the flour and mix thoroughly; then add the oats and combine until the mixture resembles coarse pebbles.

3. Spread the mixture evenly on a cookie sheet and bake for 10 to 15 minutes or until golden, fragrant, and a bit crunchy. Meanwhile, prepare the soup.

Soup

1. Place all the ingredients in a 5-quart pot over high heat. Cover and bring to a boil, then reduce the heat to low and simmer for about 15 minutes. Remove from the heat and take out the cinnamon sticks.

2. Place 4 cups of the soup in a blender and blend until smooth. Return to the pot and stir through. Ladle into bowls, top with the crumble, and serve.

> **Hands-on prep time:** 35 minutes
> **Cook time:** 20 minutes
> **Total time:** 45 minutes
> **Makes** about 8 cups soup plus 1 cup crumble

Ingredients

Crumble Topping

¼ **cup butter** (softened)
6 **Tbsp sugar**
½ **tsp vanilla**
½ **cup unbleached white flour**
½ **cup quick oats**

Soup

4 **cups water**
14 **cups peeled, chopped apple** (about 4 pounds)
¾ **cup sugar**
4 **sticks cinnamon**
1 **tsp pumpkin pie spice**
2 **Tbsp butter**
1 **Tbsp vanilla**

Strawberry Shortcake Soup

My daughters love strawberries. And after having a rather dry strawberry shortcake dessert one night, we felt compelled to make this delicious dessert soup, which saturates simple buttery biscuits with a luscious strawberry-balsamic reduction. Slathered with whipped cream and fresh strawberries, this is definitely one of those sinful soups we only wish we could make every day.

Procedure

Shortcake

1. Preheat the oven to 350°F.

2. Place the flours, sugar, and baking powder in a 3-quart bowl and mix thoroughly. Cut the butter into the mixture using a pastry cutter or your hands until the mixture resembles coarse pebbles. Add the milk and mix until the ingredients are just combined. Set aside for 5 minutes while you slice the strawberries for the soup (see next page).

3. Roll out the pastry mixture on a floured surface until it is about ¾ inch thick. Then, using a cookie cutter or the top of a drinking glass, cut out biscuits in whatever shape you like. (If using very small cutters, roll the dough out to ¼ to ½ inch thick.)

4. Place the biscuit cutouts on a cookie sheet 2 inches apart to allow them to expand. Bake for about 10 to 15 minutes until the bottoms are golden. (If your shortcakes are very small, reduce the baking time to 8 to 12 minutes.) Cool for 5 to 10 minutes before serving. Meanwhile, prepare the soup (see next page).

Whipped Cream

Place all the ingredients in a large deep bowl. With an electric mixer, beat for a few minutes on high until the cream holds its shape. Chill until ready to serve.

> **Hands-on prep time:** 30 minutes
> **Cook time:** 25 minutes
> **Cool time:** 5-10 minutes
> **Total time:** 40 minutes
> **Makes** about 8 cups soup plus 12 medium biscuits (2 per bowl)

Ingredients

Shortcake
1 cup whole wheat flour
1 cup unbleached white flour
¼ cup sugar
1 Tbsp baking powder
½ cup butter (softened)
¾ cup milk

Whipped Cream
1 cup whipping cream
2 Tbsp sugar
½ tsp vanilla

Ingredients

4 cups plus 3 Tbsp water

6 cups sliced fresh or frozen strawberries plus extra fresh for garnishing

1 Tbsp balsamic vinegar

¾ cup sugar

2 Tbsp cornstarch

Soup

Procedure

1. Place the 4 cups water and the strawberries, vinegar, and sugar in a 4-quart pot over high heat. Bring to a boil, reduce the heat to medium-low, cover, and simmer for 5 minutes while you prepare the whipped cream.

2. Combine the cornstarch and 3 tablespoons water to form a smooth paste. Add half of this to the soup, stirring constantly to prevent lumps from forming. Simmer for a couple of minutes before adding the remaining paste (you may not need all of it if the soup seems just thick enough; it should be neither watery nor jelly-like). Increase the heat to high and bring to a boil, then remove from heat and set aside. Add a little extra water if you need to.

3. Ladle the soup into shallow bowls. Either place 1 or 2 shortcakes in the center of each soup or split a shortcake in half, fill with whipped cream and strawberries (like a sandwich), and place in the center of each soup. Garnish with whipped cream and the remaining strawberry slices.

Tips/Variations

Shortcake shortcut: Instead of making shortcakes from scratch, use Pepperidge Farm mini pastry shells. Prepare according to the package directions. Remove the top of the shells, fill with whipped cream and strawberries, then replace the top, place in the center of the soup, and garnish with more strawberries and whipped cream.

Whipped cream shortcut: Use store-bought ready-whipped cream.

Whipped cream secret: If you'd like your whipped cream to hold its form well, add 1 to 2 tablespoons regular sour cream (don't use light or fat-free) and 1 tablespoon powdered sugar before beating.

Honeydew Delight
with White Chocolate Mousse

Energizing, elegant, and summery, this pretty soup is the perfect ending to a light meal. In a pinch, use vanilla whole-milk yogurt instead of the mousse. Rich in digestive enzymes, this soup can also be served as an appetizer without the mousse.

Plan ahead: Make the mousse the night before so it has time to set. Also, make the melon balls first and then use the rest of each melon for blending.

Procedure

Mousse

1. Place the silken tofu in a blender and blend until smooth. Set aside.

2. Using a double boiler, bring about a cup of water to a boil. Heat the milk over it. Remove from the heat and add the white chocolate chips. Give them a stir and cover, stirring them again every minute or so until smooth. If you need to, bring the water back to a boil, remove from the heat, then place the chocolate chips back over the water. Do this for only a minute, however, as too much heat will cause the chips to turn into one gluey mass.

3. Add the orange zest and tofu to the melted chocolate chips, combine thoroughly, and chill for 12 to 24 hours.

Soup

Place all the ingredients except the melon balls in a blender and blend until smooth. Pour the soup into bowls, garnish with 6 to 8 melon balls and a generous dollop of mousse, and serve.

> **Hands-on prep time:** 25 minutes
> **Cook time:** 5 minutes
> **Chill time:** 12-24 hours (for the mousse)
> **Total time:** 30 minutes (not including mousse setting time)
> **Makes** about 8 cups soup plus 2 cups mousse

Ingredients

White Chocolate Mousse
- **12 ounces silken tofu**
- **3 Tbsp milk**
- **2 cups white chocolate chips**
- **1 tsp finely minced or grated orange zest**

Soup
- **7 cups chilled honeydew, cut into chunks** (2 melons)
- **¼ cup granulated fructose or to taste**
- **2 Tbsp lime juice**
- **1 tsp minced or grated orange zest**
- **1 cup chilled honeydew melon balls** for garnishing
- **1 cup chilled cantaloupe melon balls** for garnishing

Broths

More than just a great way to clean out the crisper, making a broth of different vegetables, herbs, and spices deepens and draws out essential flavors and fragrances, taking your soup to the next level of deliciousness.

Italian Broth

Ideally, all Italian soups should be made with this broth. Even savory bean and grain soups can benefit from it. It offers deep, interesting flavors that only time, simmering, and quality ingredients can impart. When you taste it, you'll understand why broths create a superior soup. Simmer for longer if you like—it will only get better with time.

Procedure

Place all the ingredients in a 6-quart stockpot and bring to a boil over high heat. Reduce the heat to medium, cover, and simmer for about 1½ hours. Remove from the heat and allow to cool for a couple of hours (optional), then strain the veggies through a fine sieve or cheesecloth.

Tips/Variations

Use Italian Broth for: Homestyle Minestrone (p. 39), Oven-Roasted Vegetable Soup (p. 55), Roasted Fennel Carrot Blend (p. 83), Italian Summer Squash Soup (p. 89), Wheatberry Florentine (p. 93), Everyday Bean Chowder (p. 97), Tuscan Orzo Soup (p. 109), Pasta e Fagioli (p. 113), Wild Rice & Yam Potage (p. 117), Ribollita (p. 119), Homestyle Seitan Stew (p. 229).

Leftover veggies: Use leftover vegetables in pasta sauce or in a puréed veggie mash with butter and Braggs.

Sandwich patties: You can also make leftovers into sandwich patties. Simply combine with oats, crumbled tofu, and Spike to taste, then form into patties. Pan-fry in vegetable oil or butter until golden and crisp. Be sure to remove the rosemary, thyme, and bay leaf first!

Hands-on prep time: 20-30 minutes
Cook time: 1 hour 30 minutes
Total time: 2 hours (not including cooling time)
Makes about 10 cups

Ingredients

- 12 cups water
- 1 large red onion, chopped
- 1 leek, chopped
- 6 cloves garlic, crushed*
- 1 red bell pepper, roughly chopped
- 3 carrots, roughly chopped
- 4 stalks celery, roughly chopped (including leaves)
- 4 roma tomatoes, roughly chopped (or one 19-ounce can)
- 3 long sprigs fresh Italian parsley
- 2 sprigs fresh thyme
- 1 sprig fresh rosemary
- 1 bay leaf
- 1 tsp salt
- ¼ tsp whole black peppercorns
- One 3-ounce chunk parmesan cheese
- ¼ cup sherry

*Use a rolling pin or the flat side of a substantial knife.

Basic Veggie Broth

Ingredients

1 Tbsp oil

1 large onion, quartered

4 large garlic cloves, chopped

7-8 cups roughly chopped mixed vegetables
(like potato, carrot, and celery)

3 bay leaves

15 cups water

Good Broth Veggies

- Cabbage
- Carrot
- Celery
- Fennel
- Garlic
- Leek
- Onion
- Parsnip
- Potato
- Tomato
- Turnip
- Yam

This is a good basic broth formula that you can play around with according to what you've got. I consider it the ideal "end-of-the-week" recipe because by Friday I seem to have a little bit of everything in the crisper. Making broth unites those odds and ends and turns them into something cohesive. This recipe can be used for just about any soup in place of water.

Procedure

Heat the oil in a 6-quart pot over high heat. Add the onion and garlic and sauté for a few minutes until they begin to brown. Add the remaining ingredients, cover, and bring to a boil. Reduce the heat to medium and simmer for 40 minutes to an hour. Remove from the heat, allow to cool for a couple of hours (optional), then strain the veggies through a fine sieve or cheesecloth.

Asian Broth Variation

Use sesame or peanut oil. Add one 3-inch piece of ginger (chopped), 1-2 cups chopped shiitake mushrooms, and 3 star anise. You can also add 2 teaspoons of hijiki or arame seaweed, a couple of tablespoons of miso of choice, and a splash of rice vinegar. If you're going Thai, toss in a stalk of lemongrass, a whole fresh chili, a handful of Thai basil or cilantro, and/or a few kaffir lime leaves.

Use in place of water for: Lotus Root Udon Noodle Soup (p. 123), Teriyaki Soup (p. 125), Vegetable Pho (p. 129), Watercress Rice Noodle Soup (p. 139), Wonton Min (p. 143), Soupe de Seitan l'Orange (p. 181), Spicy Lotus Root Soup (p. 201), Napa Mushroom Soup (p. 203).

Leftover veggies: Roughly purée the strained veggies with a splash each of soy sauce, rice vinegar, and toasted sesame oil. Then combine with green onion and minced water chestnut. Use this as a filling for wonton dumplings or potstickers.

Vegetarian Chicken Broth Variation

In your mixed vegetables, be sure to include 1 roughly chopped yam and 2 roughly chopped parsnips. You'll also want to add 3 sprigs fresh thyme, 1 sprig fresh summer savory, 1 teaspoon poultry seasoning, ½ teaspoon whole black peppercorns, 3 tablespoons nutritional yeast, and 1 tablespoon vegetarian worcestershire sauce (optional).

Use in place of water for: Matzoh Ball Soup (p. 31), Vegetarian Chicken Noodle (p. 37), Young Vegetable Chowder (p. 57), Hearty Root Vegetable Chowder (p. 63), Roasted Celeriac Parsnip Soup (p. 85), Everyday Bean Chowder (p. 97), Wild Rice & Yam Potage (p. 117), Daydream Soup (p. 151), Mac 'n Cheese Soup (p. 153), Volcano Soup (p. 157), October Harvest (p. 163), Gumbo (p. 227), Hungarian Goulash (p. 231), Chilled Cauliflower Curry (p. 251).

Mushroom Broth Variation

In your mixed vegetables, be sure to include 4 cups roughly chopped mushrooms (stems included), 2 roughly chopped parsnips, and 1 chopped leek. You'll also want to add 1 teaspoon dried sage, a few sprigs fresh chervil, thyme, or rosemary, ½ teaspoon whole black peppercorns, and ¾ cup sherry.

Use in place of water for: Amazing Cream of Mushroom (p. 29), Oven-Roasted Vegetable Soup (p. 55), Mighty Mushroom Barley Soup (p. 105), Winter Mushroom Alfredo (p. 115), Wild Rice & Yam Potage (p. 117), Homestyle Seitan Stew (p. 229), Hungarian Goulash (p. 231), Seitan Stroganoff (p. 233).

Leftover veggies: Use the strained vegetables in homemade tofu or grain burgers or a veggie loaf or pâté.

> **Hands-on prep time:** 10 minutes
> **Cook time:** 45-60 minutes
> **Cool time:** 2 hours (optional)
> **Total time:** About 1 hour (not including cooling time)
> **Makes** about 10-12 cups

Broth tips ...

Don't throw out your odds and ends! When cooking in general, don't toss out parsley or mushroom stems, cabbage and fennel cores, celery leaves, or other odds and ends. Save them, and every few days toss them into a pot with some water and simmer for an hour. Add a chopped potato or carrot to round it out if you need to.

Broth for more than just soup: Use broth instead of water to boil grains like rice or quinoa, or to make vegetarian gravy and other homemade sauces.

Enrich the flavor: To create a richer broth, add a chunk of parmesan cheese, a few tablespoons of nutritional yeast, and/or a splash of vegetarian worcestershire sauce or vinegar (such as balsamic, sherry, or champagne). A couple of tablespoons of miso or a veggie bouillon cube or two can also embellish the flavor—as can a couple of veggie burgers crumbled up into the broth.

Garnishes at a Glance

Whether it's salsa or chutney, croutons or crostinis,
the simple garnishes in this chapter can make your
soup a spectacular, mouthwatering meal.

Three Crostini Variations

Crostinis make great use of stale bread. They can also make a soup more exciting and substantial. Generally, crostinis become quite hard in the oven. My daughter Satya describes each as "one giant, flavorful crouton." Place one or two crostinis directly into a bowl of soup just before serving and let them soften as they soak up the broth.

Roasted Garlic Crostini

1-day-old baguette, sliced just under 1 inch thick

2 bulbs roasted garlic*

¾ cup shaved or thinly sliced Asiago
   or parmesan cheese (about 4 ounces)

2 Tbsp minced fresh sage

*See Roasting Garlic, p 11.

Procedure

Preheat the oven to 375°F. Spread the bread slices on a baking tray and smear a clove of roasted garlic on each. Then top with cheese and a pinch of sage. Bake for about 10 to 15 minutes or until the edges of the bread are golden and crisp and the cheese is melted.

Chèvre-Tomato Crostini

1-day-old baguette, sliced just under 1 inch thick

¾ cup chèvre (soft goat cheese) (about 6 ounces)

18 whole teardrop or grape tomatoes or halved
   cherry tomatoes

Procedure

Preheat the oven to 375°F. Spread the bread slices on a baking tray and smear each with about 1 teaspoon chèvre. Then top with a tomato (if halved, place flat side down). Bake for 10 to 15 minutes or until the bread is golden and crisp at the edges, the chèvre becomes very soft and creamy, and the tomato has shriveled slightly.

Feta-Red Onion Crostini

1-day-old baguette, sliced just under 1 inch thick

¾ cup finely sliced feta cheese (about 4 ounces)

¼ cup slivered red onion

Procedure

Preheat the oven to 375°F. Spread the bread slices on a baking tray and top with feta and 3 or 4 slivers of onion. Bake for 10 to 15 minutes or until the edges of bread are golden and crisp, the cheese perspires, and the onion wilts.

Tips/Variations

All go well with: Homestyle Minestrone (p. 39), Oven-Roasted Vegetable Soup (p. 55), Roasted Tomato Herb Soup (p. 81), Italian Summer Squash Soup (p. 89), Tuscan Orzo Soup (p. 109), Pasta e Fagioli (p. 113), Winter Mushroom Alfredo (p. 115), Alphabet Soup (p. 149).

Hands-on prep time: 5-10 minutes per recipe
Bake time: 5-15 minutes per recipe (5 minutes for a softer crostini, 10-15 for crunchy)
Total time: No more than 25 minutes
Makes 18 per recipe

Crouton Variations

Everyone in my family has an affinity for croutons. Sometimes I even think soups and salads are mere vehicles for them. Homemade croutons offer plenty of room for experimentation, so feel free to try different seasonings, like madras curry powder, crumbled dried rosemary with minced garlic, or a sprinkle of caraway seeds with melted butter. You can also use different types of bread, like pumpernickel or rye, focaccia, or even a hearty raisin-nut loaf.

Italian Croutons

2 Tbsp oil
¼ tsp salt
Fresh-ground black pepper
½ tsp granulated garlic
1½ tsp Italian seasoning
One 1-pound loaf crusty Italian bread
    (preferably stale, unsliced)

Procedure

Preheat the oven to 375°F. Combine the first 5 ingredients in a large mixing bowl. Cut or tear the bread into chunky 2x2-inch pieces, place them in the mixing bowl, and toss until coated with seasonings. Place the seasoned bread chunks on a baking tray and bake for 10 to 15 minutes until golden and crunchy, turning once halfway.

Tips/Variations

Cheesy variation: Add 2 tablespoons grated parmesan cheese.

> **Hands-on prep time:** 5 minutes
> **Bake time:** 15 minutes
> **Total time:** 20 minutes
> **Makes** about 4 cups

Savory Croutons

3 slices wholegrain bread, cubed
Oil spray
1 tsp Spike, lemon pepper, or other seasoning salt
2 tsp nutritional yeast (optional)

Spicy Croutons

3 slices wholegrain bread, cubed
Oil spray
1 tsp Cajun or Mexican seasoning (salted)

Procedure *(for both Savory and Spicy Croutons)*

Preheat the oven to 375°F. Spread the bread cubes on a baking tray and spray liberally with oil until well coated. Sprinkle with the seasonings and toss. Bake for 10 minutes until golden and crunchy, turning once halfway.

> **Hands-on prep time:** 5 minutes per recipe
> **Bake time:** 10 minutes per recipe
> **Total time:** 15 minutes per recipe
> **Makes** 1½-2 cups per recipe

Complementary Crackers

A solution for snackers: healthy homemade crackers. I've been making these for decades, and both kids and adults love them. They make a splendid accompaniment to all kinds of soups, salads, and dips.

Savory Pita Crisps

Two 8-inch whole wheat pita breads

Half a lemon (rub flat side onto bread, squeezing lightly to release juice)

Oil spray

2 tsp nutritional yeast

1 tsp Spike

Sprinkle of cayenne pepper (optional)

Mediterranean Pita Crisps

Two 8-inch whole wheat pita breads

Oil spray

2 tsp Italian seasoning or minced fresh rosemary

½ tsp coarse salt

Fresh-ground black pepper to taste

2 tsp finely minced garlic

2 tsp parmesan cheese (optional)

Chili Lime Tortilla Crisps

4 whole wheat flour or corn tortillas

Half a lime (rub flat side onto tortilla, squeezing lightly to release juice)

Oil spray

1-2 tsp chili powder (depends on heat and saltiness)

1 minced fresh jalapeño (optional)

¼ cup finely minced cilantro (optional)

Procedure *(for all 3 crisps)*

Preheat the oven to 350°F. Place the breads or tortillas on a cutting board and spray generously with oil. Sprinkle equal amounts of the seasonings on each piece, then slice each into 8 triangles. Transfer the triangles to a baking sheet and bake for 5 to 10 minutes or until crisp.

Tips/Variations

Savory and Mediterranean Pita Crisps go well with: Any non-Asian soup.

Chili Lime Tortilla Crisps go well with: Tex-Mex Cauliflower Soup (p. 51), Albondigas (p. 65), Cheesy Corn Chipotle Chowder (p. 67), Fiesta Black Bean Soup (p. 103), Nacho Bean Soup (p. 161), Hearty Chili (p. 225), Gumbo (p. 227), Avocado Lime Soup (p. 253).

For kids: Use a sprinkle of mild chili powder and grated pepper jack cheese on pitas or tortillas.

Hands-on prep time: 5 minutes per recipe
Bake time: 10 minutes per recipe
Total time: 15 minutes per recipe
Makes 16 pita crisps or 32 tortilla crisps per recipe

Quinoa Pilaf

This is a staple dish in our household, not only because it complements so many dishes, but also because quinoa is a high-energy food that's perfect for athletes like my children. Easy to digest, quinoa has a wealth of calcium, iron, B vitamins, and vitamin E. It also strengthens the entire body, especially the heart and kidneys. Because it's actually a seed, quinoa is an incredible 16% protein—more than any other grain.

1½ cups quinoa, rinsed

3 cups water

1 tsp salt or to taste

½ cup finely chopped carrot

½ cup finely chopped tomato (1-2 roma tomatoes)

½ cup finely chopped Japanese or English cucumber

¼ cup minced red onion and/or chopped green onion

¼ cup minced Italian parsley or cilantro

2 Tbsp lemon juice

Procedure

1. Place the quinoa, water, and salt in a 2-quart pot and bring to a boil over high heat. Boil for 2 minutes, then reduce the heat to medium-low, cover, and simmer for 15 to 20 minutes until no water remains. Fluff with a fork and set aside to cool for 30 to 60 minutes.

2. Place the quinoa with the remaining ingredients in a 2-quart mixing bowl and combine well. Salt to taste and serve.

Tips/Variations

Goes well with: Sopa de Tortilla (p. 41) and too many others to list.

Hands-on prep time: 10 minutes
Cook time: 25 minutes
Cool time: 30-60 minutes
Total time: 60-90 minutes
Makes about 4½ cups

Smoky Tempeh

Kids and non-vegetarians especially love this low-fat veggie bacon spinoff. Not only is it fantastic atop a brothy Italian or homestyle soup, but it's also great with a creamy potato salad or inside TLTs (tempeh-lettuce-tomato sandwiches).

Oil spray

One 8-ounce package tempeh, thinly sliced

2 Tbsp Bragg Liquid Aminos or tamari

1½ tsp liquid smoke

2 Tbsp nutritional yeast (optional)

Procedure

1. Spray a medium skillet with the oil spray and place over medium-high heat. Add the tempeh and spray a bit more oil, making sure the tempeh is nicely coated. Cook for about 5 minutes, turning a few times, until both sides are browned.

2. Add the Braggs or tamari and liquid smoke and cook for a couple of more minutes, turning continuously until the tempeh has absorbed all the liquid. Sprinkle with the nutritional yeast (optional) and toss until coated. Remove from the heat and serve.

Tips/Variations

Goes well with: Cream of Asparagus (p. 25), Fabulous French Onion (p. 35), Russian Sweet & Sour (p. 59), Italian Summer Squash Soup (p. 89), Wheatberry Florentine (p. 93), Hearty Fall Lentil Soup (p. 95), Everyday Bean Chowder (p. 97), Caribbean Yucca Bean Chowder (p. 99), Tuscan Orzo Soup (p. 109), Butternut Lentil Soup (p. 193), Carrot Leek Bisque (p. 199), Red Lentil Sauerkraut Soup (p. 207), Valentine Soup (p. 209).

> **Hands-on prep time:** 3 minutes
> **Cook time:** 7 minutes
> **Total time:** 10 minutes
> **Makes** about 2 cups

Minted Couscous

Light and lovely, this simple side dish goes beautifully with many of the recipes in this book. You can even make it the luscious centerpiece of a soup or stew to create a complete meal.

2¼ cups water

1¼ tsp salt or to taste

1½ cups couscous

¾ cup minced red onion

1 cup minced mint leaves

8 pitted, minced medjool dates

1½ Tbsp apple cider vinegar

1½ Tbsp oil

Procedure

1. Place the water and salt in a 2-quart pot and bring to a boil over high heat. Add the couscous (make sure the grains are quite level), cover, and remove from the heat. Let sit for about 5 minutes. Fluff with a fork. If serving on its own, let cool for an hour or until room temperature (no need to cool if adding to a soup).

2. Place the couscous with the remaining ingredients in a 2-quart mixing bowl and combine well. Salt to taste and serve.

Tips/Variations

Goes well with: Moroccan Chickpea Chowder (p. 101) and too many others to list.

> **Hands-on prep time:** 5-10 minutes
> **Cook time:** 5 minutes
> **Cool time:** About 1 hour
> **Total time:** Just over an hour
> **Makes** about 4½ cups

Teriyaki Tofu

This recipe—or some variation of it—gets made at least once a week at our house. It's simple and tasty and goes well with plenty of dishes. You can garnish with toasted sesame seeds, cilantro, or green onion.

1½ cups extra-firm tofu, cut in your favorite shape
¼ cup brown sugar
3 Tbsp soy sauce
2 Tbsp minced or slivered ginger

Procedure

Place all the ingredients in a medium skillet over medium-high heat. Cook for about 5 minutes, stirring often, until all the sauce is absorbed and the tofu looks caramelized. Remove from the heat.

Tips/Variations

Goes well with: Kabocha Ginger Soup (p. 75), Wasabi Green Pea Soup (p. 79), Lotus Root Udon Noodle Soup (p. 123), Teriyaki Soup (p. 125), Thai Carrot Soup (p. 127), Vegetable Pho (p. 129), Watercress Rice Noodle Soup (p. 139), I Love Peanut Butter Soup (p. 155), Spicy Lotus Root Soup (p. 201).

Hands-on prep time: 10 minutes
Cook time: 5 minutes
Total time: 15 minutes
Makes about 1½ cups

Seitan l'Orange

This luscious Szechwan-inspired dish is equally delicious made with tofu. If you like it hot, double the chili.

2 Tbsp toasted sesame oil
3 Tbsp grated orange zest (2 oranges)
1 Tbsp minced garlic (2-3 cloves)
8 ounces seitan, sliced
¼ cup orange marmalade
2 Tbsp brown sugar
2 Tbsp soy sauce
½ tsp minced fresh chili (optional)

Procedure

Heat the oil in a medium skillet over high heat. Add the zest and sauté for a couple of minutes until it begins to brown. Add the garlic and seitan and sauté for a minute. Mix together the marmalade, sugar, soy sauce, and chili (optional) and pour over seitan. Stir to coat the seitan and sauté for a few more minutes until caramelized. Remove from the heat.

Tips/Variations

Goes well with: Winter Squash Potato Soup (p. 61), Lotus Root Udon Noodle Soup (p. 123), Vegetable Pho (p. 129), Malaysian Peanut Soup (p. 131), Watercress Rice Noodle Soup (p. 139), Wonton Min (p. 143), Soupe de Seitan l'Orange (p. 181).

Hands-on prep time: 5-10 minutes
Cook time: About 7 minutes
Total time: 15 minutes
Makes about 2 cups

Seasoned TVP Nuggets

I often recommend this recipe to anyone trying to feed a big family on a budget. Simple and economical, TVP (textured vegetable protein) has a somewhat chewy, hearty texture that's perfect for stews and chowders. It's also delicious with roasted veggies and a buttery turnip mash. You can find TVP in most health food, bulk, and gourmet grocery stores.

1½ cups dried TVP chunks

Enough water to cover the TVP

3 Tbsp butter or oil

1 tsp Spike or to taste

2 tsp lemon juice

½ tsp liquid smoke (optional)

Procedure

Place the TVP and water in a 2-quart pot and bring to a boil over high heat. Reduce the heat to medium, cover, and simmer for a few minutes until most of the water is absorbed and the TVP is soft. Pour out any remaining water, then add the remaining ingredients. Sauté the TVP for a few minutes, stirring often, until slightly golden and encrusted with the Spike. Remove from the heat.

Tips/Variations

Goes well with: Amazing Cream of Mushroom (p. 29), Homestyle Minestrone (p. 39), Russian Sweet & Sour (p. 59), Hearty Root Vegetable Chowder (p. 63), Everyday Bean Chowder (p. 97), Wild Rice & Yam Potage (p. 117), Mac 'n Cheese Soup (p. 153), I Love Peanut Butter Soup (p. 155), Volcano Soup (p. 157), Red Lentil Sauerkraut Soup (p. 207), Hungarian Goulash (p. 231).

Hands-on prep time: 5 minutes
Cook time: 10 minutes
Total time: 15 minutes
Makes about 2 cups

Apple Radish Salsa

Refreshing and sophisticated, this light, aromatic salsa is a colorful and nutritious addition to any summer soup, snack, or meal.

¾ cup peeled, diced apple (like Granny Smith or pink lady)

1 cup roughly peeled, finely diced seedless cucumber

¼ cup minced radish

½ cup minced fresh mint leaves

2 Tbsp minced chives (use scissors)

3 Tbsp lemon juice

½ tsp salt

1 tsp honey

Procedure

Combine all the ingredients in a 1-quart bowl and chill until needed.

Tips/Variations

Goes well with: Easy Zucchini Bisque (p. 87), Olive Avocado Cream (p. 197), Greek Goddess (p. 241), Minted Pea Bisque (p. 249), Avocado Lime Soup (p. 253).

Total prep time: 15 minutes
Makes just over 2 cups

Summer Salsa

This luscious salsa works well with soups, salads, corn chips, veggie burritos, or grilled tofu fillets. It can even be used as a little side salad in itself. Add a minced kaffir lime leaf whenever you can.

1 cup finely diced mango or pineapple

½ cup diced tomato

½ cup minced radish

1 cup minced cilantro or mint leaves

2 Tbsp minced vidalia or other sweet onion

2 Tbsp lime juice

½ tsp salt

Procedure

Combine all the ingredients in a 1-quart bowl and chill until needed.

Tips/Variations

Goes well with: Wasabi Green Pea Soup (p. 79), Easy Zucchini Bisque (p. 87), Fiesta Black Bean Soup (p. 103), Thai Carrot Soup (p. 127), Raw Energizer (p. 217), Everfresh Soup (p. 219), Minted Pea Bisque (p. 249), Avocado Lime Soup (p. 253).

Total prep time: 10 minutes
Makes about 2 cups

Pear Chutney

Perfect for Indian curries, this delightful condiment is equally delicious warm or chilled.

2 ripe pears, finely chopped (peeled or unpeeled)
¾ cup chopped walnuts
2 Tbsp currants
¼ cup brown sugar
2 Tbsp water
¼ cup minced celery plus leaves (optional)

Procedure

Place all the ingredients except the celery in a small saucepan over high heat and bring to a boil. Reduce the heat to medium, cover, and simmer for about 15 minutes, stirring occasionally, until most of the liquid has evaporated. Add the celery (optional) and remove from the heat.

Tips/Variations

Goes well with: Mellow Potato Curry (p. 49), Hearty Root Vegetable Chowder (p. 63), Mulligatawny (p. 69), Roasted Celeriac Parsnip Soup (p. 85), Easy Dhal (p. 111), October Harvest (p. 163), Waldorf Chowder (p. 183).

Hands-on prep time: 5 minutes
Cook time: 20 minutes
Total time: 25 minutes
Makes about 2 cups

Mango Chutney

Light and luscious, this beautiful sweet and spicy chutney is the embodiment of simplicity. In addition to soup, it's also wonderful with crispy samosas, spring rolls, or tempura-battered vegetables.

2½ cups chopped mango (about 2 large mangoes)
½ tsp minced fresh chili or red chili flakes
1 tsp minced ginger
2 Tbsp honey or sugar
¼ cup fresh mint leaves (tightly packed)
1 Tbsp lemon juice

Procedure

Place all the ingredients except ½ cup of the mango in a blender and blend until smooth. Transfer to a serving dish, then dice the remaining ½ cup mango and stir it into the purée. Chill until ready to serve.

Tips/Variations

Goes well with: Winter Squash Potato Soup (p. 61), Mulligatawny (p. 69), Garnet Yam Bisque (p. 77), Fiesta Black Bean Soup (p. 103), Thai Carrot Soup (p. 127), Easy Indian Curry (p. 137), October Harvest (p. 163), Minted Pea Bisque (p. 249), Avocado Lime Soup (p. 253).

Total prep time: 5-10 minutes
Makes just over 2 cups

Valentine Slaw

This lovely bittersweet slaw contains properties that protect, nourish, and strengthen your heart. Radicchio is slightly bitter, so use red cabbage if you prefer.

½ cup peeled, grated apple (like Granny Smith or pink lady)
½ cup peeled, grated beet
¼ cup finely shredded radicchio or red cabbage

Procedure

Combine all the ingredients in a 1-quart bowl and chill until needed.

Tips/Variations

Goes well with: Wasabi Green Pea Soup (p. 79), Roasted Celeriac Parsnip Soup (p. 85), Easy Zucchini Bisque (p. 87), Olive Avocado Cream (p. 197), Valentine Soup (p. 209), Raw Energizer (p. 217), Minted Pea Bisque (p. 249), Avocado Lime Soup (p. 253).

Total prep time: 5 minutes
Makes just over 1 cup

Slimming Slaw

This tasty slaw is a wonderful remedy for excessive weight gain, water retention, and low energy. Use it to dress up any of the soups listed below or to top baked potatoes or brown rice.

1½ cups julienned cucumber
1 Tbsp nutritional yeast
¼ tsp salt
¼ tsp cayenne or red chili flakes
2 tsp flax oil
2 tsp apple cider vinegar

Procedure

Combine all the ingredients in a 1-quart bowl and chill until needed.

Tips/Variations

Goes well with: Wasabi Green Pea Soup (p. 79), Easy Zucchini Bisque (p. 87), Teriyaki Soup (p. 125), Olive Avocado Cream (p. 197), Spring Detox (p. 205), Fat Burner (p. 215), Raw Energizer (p. 217), Greek Goddess (p. 241).

Total prep time: 5-10 minutes
Makes about 1½ cups

Daikon Slaw

Though often an acquired taste, daikon has long been valued for its peppery flavor, crunchy texture, and incredible health benefits. A natural immune booster and decongestant, this enzyme-rich vegetable also makes a wonderful digestive aid.

1½ cups peeled, julienned or grated daikon radish
1 Tbsp Bragg Liquid Aminos or tamari
1 Tbsp apple cider vinegar
¼ tsp minced fresh chili or red chili flakes

Procedure

Combine all the ingredients in a 1-quart bowl and chill until ready to serve.

Tips/Variations

Goes well with: Wasabi Green Pea Soup (p. 79), Lotus Root Udon Noodle Soup (p. 123), Teriyaki Soup (p. 125), Szechwan Dumpling Soup (p. 173), Wasabi Noodle Soup (p. 213), Minted Pea Bisque (p. 249).

Total prep time: 5 minutes
Makes about 1½ cups

Herb-Infused Oil

A fresh herb oil makes an elegant finishing touch on a variety of soups, especially smooth blended ones. You can use basil, chives, parsley, or tarragon—or any combination. Even toss in a clove of garlic if you like. Use leftover oil on salads or for bread dipping.

½ cup olive oil
½ cup fresh herbs of choice

Procedure

Place all the ingredients in a blender and blend until the oil is green and filmy. Strain the mixture twice through a fine sieve or cheesecloth and discard the pulp. You can use the oil right away, though it will have a fuller flavor and aroma after 12 hours. Keeps for a week at room temperature.

Tips/Variations

Goes well with: Oven-Roasted Vegetable Soup (p. 55), Creamy Cashew Soup (p. 73), Roasted Fennel Carrot Blend (p. 83), Roasted Celeriac Parsnip Soup (p. 85), Italian Summer Squash Soup (p. 89), Parsnip Apple Bisque (p. 195), Carrot Leek Bisque (p. 199).

Total prep time: 5 minutes
Makes about ½ cup

Cashew Sour Cream

If you're sensitive to dairy products, you needn't feel deprived of sour cream with this great vegan garnish.

½ cup raw cashews

½ cup cold water

⅔ cup extra-firm silken tofu

1 tsp balsamic vinegar

¼ tsp salt

Procedure

Place all the ingredients in a blender and blend until smooth. Transfer to a small serving dish and chill for 30 minutes or longer if desired.

Tips/Variations

Goes well with: Sopa de Tortilla (p. 41), Tex-Mex Cauliflower Soup (p. 51), Russian Sweet & Sour (p. 59), Fiesta Black Bean Soup (p. 103), Lemony Lentil Chard Soup (p. 107), Hungarian Goulash (p. 231), Spring Borscht (p. 255).

> **Total prep time:** 2 minutes
> **Makes** about 1 cup

Fresh Dill Cream

Though wonderful with dill, this easy garnish also works well with other fresh herbs, like cilantro, basil, or mint. You can also blend it with a few sun-dried tomatoes, roasted red peppers, or a teaspoon of prepared horseradish.

12 ounces silken tofu or 1½ cups sour cream

½ tsp salt

½ tsp garlic powder

3 Tbsp eggless mayonnaise (only if using tofu)

3 Tbsp minced fresh dill (or 1-2 tsp dried)

Procedure

Place all the ingredients in a blender and blend until smooth. Transfer to a small serving dish and chill until needed.

Tips/Variations

Goes well with: Russian Sweet & Sour (p. 59), Roasted Tomato Herb Soup (p. 81), Hungarian Goulash (p. 231), Cocktail Tomato Soup (p. 243), Spring Borscht (p. 255).

> **Total prep time:** 3 minutes
> **Makes** about 1½ cups

Veggie Cream Cheese

Get your kids eating vegetable-packed soups with this enticing garnish. Cream cheese works like a charm!

1 cup cream cheese, cut in small cubes
2 Tbsp water
¼ tsp salt
8 chopped sun-dried tomatoes (marinated in oil)
¼ cup fresh Italian parsley or basil (packed)
¼ cup red or green bell pepper
1 Tbsp red onion
1 clove garlic

Procedure

Place all the ingredients in a blender and blend until quite smooth. Transfer to a small serving dish and chill until needed.

Tips/Variations

Goes well with: Homestyle Minestrone (p. 39), Roasted Tomato Herb Soup (p. 81), Italian Summer Squash Soup (p. 89), Pasta e Fagioli (p. 113), Alphabet Soup (p. 149).

> **Total prep time:** 5 minutes
> **Makes** just over 1 cup

Avocado Mousse

Cooling, energizing, and beautifully silken, this easy garnish can double as a light guacamole or salad dressing.

1 cup ripe avocado (1-2 avocados)
2 roughly chopped green onions
1½ tsp ground coriander
¼ tsp salt or to taste
⅓ cup water
¼ cup lime juice
2 tsp honey

Procedure

Place all the ingredients in a blender and blend until smooth and creamy. Transfer to a small serving bowl, cover, and chill until serving.

Tips/Variations

Variations: Spice it up with a teaspoon of minced fresh chili or red chili flakes. Cool it down with ½ cup cilantro or mint leaves.

Goes well with: Fiesta Black Bean Soup (p. 103), Everfresh Soup (p. 219), Cocktail Tomato Soup (p. 243), Gazpacho (p. 257).

> **Total prep time:** 5 minutes
> **Makes** just over 1 cup

Index

C

H

T

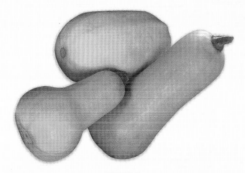

U

V

Wai Lana YOGAROMA™

NATURAL SOAP

Patchouli

HAND ✱ MADE

Wai Lana YOGAROMA

MINERAL BATH

Orange-Cinnamon

Wai Lana YOGAROMA

MINERAL BATH SALTS

Vanilla

HAND ✱ MADE

Wai Lana YOGAROMA

Wai Lana YOGAROMA

BATH OIL

Monoi de Tahiti

HAND ✱ MADE

wailana.com

For quality products:

▸ Yoga & Fitness
▸ Healthy Living
▸ Green Products